Informing the legislative debate since 1914 _____

National Security Letters in Foreign Intelligence Investigations: Legal Background

Charles Doyle
Senior Specialist in American Public Law

November 22, 2013

Congressional Research Service

7-5700

www.crs.gov

RL33320

Summary

Five federal statutes authorize intelligence officials to request certain business record information in connection with national security investigations. The authority to issue these national security letters (NSLs) is comparable to the authority to issue administrative subpoenas. The USA PATRIOT Act expanded the authority under four of the NSL statutes and created the fifth. Thereafter, the authority has been reported to have been widely used. Prospects of its continued use dimmed, however, after two lower federal courts held that the lack of judicial review and the absolute confidentiality requirements in one of the statutes rendered it constitutionally suspect.

A report by the Department of Justice's Inspector General (IG) found that in its pre-amendment use of expanded USA PATRIOT Act authority the FBI had "used NSLs in violation of applicable NSL statutes, Attorney General Guidelines, and internal FBI policies," but that no criminal laws had been broken. A year later, a second IG report confirmed the findings of the first, and noted the corrective measures taken in response. A third IG report, critical of the FBI's use of exigent letters and informal NSL alternatives, noted that the practice had been stopped and related problems addressed.

The USA PATRIOT Improvement and Reauthorization Act (H.R. 3199), P.L. 109-177, and its companion, P.L. 109-178, amended the five NSL sections to expressly provide for judicial review of both the NSLs and the confidentiality requirements that attend them. The sections have also been made explicitly judicially enforceable and sanctions recognized for failure to comply with an NSL request or to breach NSL confidentiality requirements with the intent to obstruct justice. The use of the authority has been made subject to greater congressional oversight. Following amendment, a federal district court found the amended procedure contrary to the demands of the First Amendment. The U.S. Court of Appeals for the Second Circuit, however, ruled that the amended statutes could withstand constitutional scrutiny, if the government confined itself to a procedure which requires (1) notice to the recipient of its option to object to a secrecy requirement; (2) upon recipient objection, prompt judicial review at the government's petition and burden; and (3) meaningful judicial review without conclusive weight afforded a government certification of risk. Using this procedure, the district court upheld continuation of the *Doe* nondisclosure requirement following an ex parte, in camera hearing and granted the plaintiff's motion for an unclassified, redacted summary of the government declaration on which the court's decision was based. More recently, a district court in the Ninth Circuit agreed the amended nondisclosure and judicial review provisions were constitutionally defective, but could not agree to the Second Circuit's narrowing construction or that the NSL statute could be saved by severing the deficient disclosure provisions. The district court stayed its order enjoining issuance of further NSLs or enforcement of any accompanying nondisclosure provisions, however, pending appeal to the Ninth Circuit.

The text of the five provisions—Section 1114(a)(5) of the Right to Financial Privacy Act (12 U.S.C. 3414(a)(5)); Sections 626 and 627 of the Fair Credit Reporting Act (15 U.S.C. 1681u, 1681v); Section 2709 of Title 18 of the *United States Code*; and Section 802 of the National Security Act (50 U.S.C. 3162)—in their amended form has been appended.

This report is available abridged—without footnotes, appendixes, and most of the citations to authority—as CRS Report RS22406, *National Security Letters in Foreign Intelligence Investigations: A Glimpse of the Legal Background and Recent Amendments*, by Charles Doyle.

Contents

Tables

Contacts

Introduction

Five statutory provisions vest government agencies responsible for certain foreign intelligence investigations (principally the Federal Bureau of Investigation (FBI)) with authority to issue written commands comparable to administrative subpoenas.[1] A National Security Letter (NSL) seeks customer and consumer transaction information in national security investigations from communications providers, financial institutions and credit agencies. Section 505 of the USA PATRIOT Act expanded the circumstances under which an NSL could be used.[2] Subsequent press accounts suggested that their use had become widespread.[3] Two lower federal courts, however, found the uncertainties, practices, and policies associated with the use of NSL authority contrary to the First Amendment right of freedom of speech, and thus brought into question the extent to which NSL authority could be used in the future.[4] The USA PATRIOT Improvement and Reauthorization Act[5] and P.L. 109-178 (S. 2271) amended the NSL statutes and related law to address some of the concerns raised by critics and the courts.[6] As a consequence, the Second Circuit dismissed one of the lower court cases as moot and remanded the other for reconsideration in light of the amendments.[7] On reconsideration, the district court opinion continued to be troubled by the First Amendment implications of the nondisclosure features of 18 U.S.C. 2709, even as amended.[8] The appellate court was comparably concerned, but concluded that the government might invoke the authority of 18 U.S.C. 2709 and 18 U.S.C. 3511 in a limited but constitutionally acceptable manner.[9] On remand under the procedure envisioned by the Second Circuit panel, the district court found a continuing need to maintain the original secrecy order, but ordered the government to provide the plaintiffs with an unclassified, redacted

---

[1] 18 U.S.C. 2709; 12 U.S.C. 3414; 15 U.S.C. 1681v; 15 U.S.C. 1681u; 50 U.S.C. 3162 (prior to recent reclassification, this section was found in 50 U.S.C. 436); the text of each is appended.

Federal administrative subpoena authority is discussed in U.S. Department of Justice, Office of Legal Policy, *Report to Congress on the Use of Administrative Subpoena Authorities by Executive Branch Agencies and Entities* [2002], available on March 6, 2006 at http://www.usdoj.gov/olp/intro.pdf; see also CRS Report RL33321, *Administrative Subpoenas in Criminal Investigations: A Brief Legal Analysis*, abridged as CRS Report RS22407, *Administrative Subpoenas in Criminal Investigations: A Sketch*, both by Charles Doyle.

[2] P.L. 1-7-56, 115 Stat. 365 (2001).

[3] From calendar year 2003 through 2005, the FBI issued approximately 44,000 NSLs containing 143,074 requests. In one investigation, it issued 9 NSLs requesting information relating to 11,000 telephone numbers. U.S. Department of Justice, Office of the Inspector General, *A Review of the Federal Bureau of Investigation's Use of National Security Letters (IG Report I)* at xviii-xix (March 2007), available on Sept. 3, 2009 at http://www.usdoj.gov/oig/special/s0703b/final.pdf. It issued another 49, 425 requests in 2006 for a total 192,499 requests over the four year period from 2003 through 2006, U.S. Department of Justice, Office of the Inspector General, *A Review of the Federal Bureau of Investigation's Use of National Security Letters (IG Report II)* at 9 (March 2008), available on Sept. 3, 2009 at http://www.usdoj.gov/oig/special/s0803b/final.pdf.

[4] *Doe v. Ashcroft*, 334 F.Supp.2d 471, 526-27 (S.D.N.Y. 2004)("the Court concludes that the compulsory, secret, and unreviewable production of information required by the FBI's application of 18 U.S.C. 2709 violates the Fourth Amendment and that the non-disclosure provision of 18 U.S.C. 2709(c) violates the First Amendment"); *Doe v. Gonzales*, 386 F.Supp.2d 66, 78-82 (D.Conn. 2005)(the court did not reach the Fourth Amendment issue). Justice Ginsburg declined to lift the stay of Connecticut court's injunction pending appeal in the Second Circuit, 126 S.Ct. 1 (2005).

[5] P.L. 109-177 (H.R. 3199), 120 Stat. 192 (2006).

[6] The appended statutes note the amendments and additions.

[7] *Doe v. Gonzales*, 449 F.3d 415 (2d Cir. 2006).

[8] *Doe v. Gonzales*, 500 F.Supp.2d 379 (S.D.N.Y. 2007).

[9] *John Doe, Inc. v. Mukasey*, 549 F.3d 861 (2d Cir. 2008).

summary of the declaration upon which the court's decision was based.[10] The result was somewhat different in the Ninth Circuit. There, too, a district court found that Section 2709(c)'s nondisclosure requirements violated the First Amendment and that Section 3511(b)(2)'s and (3)'s judicial review provisions violated the First Amendment and separation of powers principles.[11] It could not agree to the narrow construction favored by the Second Circuit, however, given the clear statutory language and equally clear congressional intent to afford the government broad, review-proof authority to issue NSL secrecy orders.[12] Nevertheless, pending appeal to the Ninth Circuit Court of Appeals, the district court stayed its order barring issuance of further NSLs and enforcement of any related nondisclosure requirements.[13]

Background

The ancestor of the first NSL letter provision is a statutory exception to privacy protections afforded by the Right to Financial Privacy Act (RFPA).[14] Its history is not particularly instructive and consists primarily of a determination that the exception in its original form should not be too broadly construed.[15] But the exception was just that, an exception. It was neither an affirmative grant of authority to request information nor a command to financial institutions to provided information when asked. It removed the restrictions on the release of customer information imposed on financial institutions by the Right to Financial Privacy Act, but it left them free to decline to comply when asked to do so.

> [I]n certain significant instances, financial institutions [had] declined to grant the FBI access to financial records in response to requests under Section 1114(a). The FBI informed the Committee that the problem occurs particularly in States which have State constitutional privacy protection provisions or State banking privacy laws. In those States, financial institutions decline to grant the FBI access because State law prohibits them from granting such access and the RFPA, since it permits but does not mandate such access, does not override State law. In such a situation, the concerned financial institutions which might otherwise desire to grant the FBI access to a customer's record will not do so, because State

---

[10] *Doe v. Holder*, 640 F.Supp.2d 517, 518-19 (S.D.N.Y. 2009); see also, *Doe v. Holder*, 665 F.Supp.2d 426, 433-34 (S.D.N.Y. 2009)(holding justified continued compliance with the nondisclosure requirement); *Doe v. Holder,*, 703 F.Supp.2d 313, 316-18 (S.D.N.Y. 2010)(lifting the nondisclosure requirements with respect to "(1) material within the scope of information that the NSL statute identifies as permissible for the FBI to obtain through the use of NSLs, and (2) material that the FBI has publicly acknowledged it has previously requested by means of NSLs," but continuing in effect the ban on disclosure of the remainder of the information sought).

[11] *In re National Security Letter*, 930 F.Supp.2d 1064, 1081 (N.D.Cal. 2013).

[12] *Id.* at 1080.

[13] *Id.* at 1081.

[14] Section 1114, P.L. 95-630, 92 Stat. 3706 (1978); now codified at 12 U.S.C. 3414(a)(1) (A), (B): "Nothing in this chapter (except sections 3415, 3417, 3418, and 3421 of this title) shall apply to the production and disclosure of financial records pursuant to requests from—(A) a Government authority authorized to conduct foreign counter- or foreign positive- intelligence activities for purposes of conducting such activities; [or] (B) the Secret Service for the purpose of conducting its protective functions (18 U.S.C. 3056; 3 U.S.C. 202, P.L.90-331, as amended)."

[15] "Section 1114 provides for special procedures in the case of foreign intelligence ... though the committee believes that some privacy protections may well be necessary for financial records sought during a foreign intelligence investigation, there are special problems in this area which make consideration of such protections in other congressional forums more appropriate. Nevertheless, the committee intends that this exemption be used only for legitimate foreign intelligence investigations: investigations proceeding only under the rubric of "national security" do not qualify. Rather this exception is available only to those U.S. Government officials specifically authorized to investigate the intelligence operations of foreign governments," H.Rept. 95-1383, at 55 (1978).

---

law does not allow such cooperation, and cooperation might expose them to liability to the customer whose records the FBI sought access. H.Rept. 99-690, at 15-6 (1986).

Congress responded with passage of the first NSL statute as an amendment to the Right to Financial Privacy Act, affirmatively giving the FBI access to financial institution records in certain foreign intelligence cases.[16] At the same time in the Electronic Communications Privacy Act, it afforded the FBI comparable access to the telephone company and other communications service provider customer information.[17] Together the two NSL provisions afforded the FBI access to communications and financial business records under limited circumstances—customer and customer transaction information held by telephone carriers and banks pertaining to a foreign power or its agents relevant to a foreign counter-intelligence investigation.[18]

Both the communications provider section and the Right to Financial Privacy Act section contained nondisclosure provisions[19] and limitations on further dissemination except pursuant of guidelines promulgated by the Attorney General.[20] Neither had an express enforcement mechanism nor identified penalties for failure to comply with either the NSL or the nondisclosure instruction.

In the mid-1990s, Congress added two more NSL provisions—one permits NSL use in connection with the investigation of government employee leaks of classified information under the National Security Act;[21] and the other grants the FBI access to credit agency records pursuant to the Fair Credit Reporting Act, under much the same conditions as apply to the records of financial institutions.[22] The FBI asked for the Fair Credit Reporting Act amendment as a threshold mechanism to enable it to make more effective use of its bank record access authority:

> FBI's right of access under the Right of Financial Privacy Act cannot be effectively used, however, until the FBI discovers which financial institutions are being utilized by the subject of a counterintelligence investigation. Consumer reports maintained by credit bureaus are a ready source of such information, but, although such report[s] are readily available to the private sector, they are not available to FBI counterintelligence investigators....
>
> FBI has made a specific showing ... that the effort to identify financial institutions in order to make use of FBI authority under the Right to Financial Privacy Act can not only be time-consuming and resource-intensive, but can also require the use of investigative techniques—such as physical and electronic surveillance, review of mail covers, and canvassing of all banks in an area—that would appear to be more intrusive than the review of credit reports. H.Rept. 104-427, at 36 (1996).[23]

---

[16] P.L. 99-569, §404, 100 Stat. 3197 (1986); 12 U.S.C. 3414(a)(5)(A)(1988 ed.).

[17] 18 U.S.C. 2709 (1988 ed.); *see also*, S.Rept. 99-541, at 43 (1986)("This provision is substantially the same as language recently reported by the Intelligence Committee as section 503 of the Intelligence Authorization Act for Fiscal Year 1987, [P.L. 99-569]").

[18] 18 U.S.C. 2709 (1988 ed.); 12 U.S.C. 3414(a)(5)(A)(1988 ed.).

[19] 18 U.S.C. 2709(c)("No wire or electronic communication service provider, or officer, employee, or agent thereof, shall disclose to any person that the Federal Bureau of Investigation has sought or obtained access to information or records under this section"); *see also*, 12 U.S.C. 3414(a)(5)(D). Note that unlike section 3486, the prohibition is neither temporary nor judicially supervised.

[20] 18 U.S.C. 2709(d)(1988 ed.); 12 U.S.C. 3414(a)(5)(B)(1988 ed.).

[21] 50 U.S.C. 3162.

[22] 15 U.S.C. 1681u.

[23] The Senate Intelligence Committee had made similar observations in a prior Congress when considering legislation (continued...)

The National Security Act NSL provision authorized access to credit and financial institution records of federal employees with security clearances who were required to give their consent as a condition for clearance.[24] Passed in the wake of the Ames espionage case, it is limited to investigations of classified information leaks. As noted at the time, "The Committee believes section 801 will serve as a deterrent to espionage for financial gain without burdening investigative agencies with unproductive recordkeeping or subjecting employees to new reporting requirements.... The Committee recognizes that consumer credit records have been notoriously inaccurate, and expects that information obtained pursuant to this section alone will not be the basis of an action or decision adverse to the interest of the employee involved."[25]

Both the Fair Credit Reporting Act section and the National Security Act section contain dissemination restrictions;[26] as well as safe harbor (immunity),[27] and nondisclosure provisions.[28] Neither has an explicit penalty for improper disclosure of the request, but the Fair Credit Reporting Act section expressly authorizes judicial enforcement.[29]

The USA PATRIOT Act amended three of the four existing NSL statutes and added a fifth. In each of the three NSL statutes available exclusively to the FBI—the Electronic Communications Privacy Act section (18 U.S.C. 2709), the Right to Financial Privacy Act section (12 U.S.C. 3414(a)(5)), and the Fair Credit Reporting Act section (15 U.S.C. 1681u). Section 505 of the USA PATRIOT Act:

- expanded FBI issuing authority beyond FBI headquarter officials to include the heads of the FBI field offices (i.e., Special Agents in Charge (SAC));

- eliminated the requirement that the record information sought pertain to a foreign power or the agent of a foreign power;

- required instead that the NSL request be relevant to an investigation to protect against international terrorism or foreign spying;

- added the caveat that no such investigation of an American can be predicated exclusively of First Amendment protected activities.[30]

The amendments allowed NSL authority to be employed more quickly (without the delays associated with prior approval from FBI headquarters) and more widely (without requiring that the information pertain to a foreign power or its agents).[31]

(...continued)

that ultimately became the National Security Amendment, H.Rept. 103-256, at 17-22 (1994).

[24] 50 U.S.C. 456 (1994 ed.).

[25] H.Rep.No.103-541 at 53-4 (1994).

[26] 15 U.S.C. 1681u(f), 50 U.S.C. 3162(e).

[27] 15 U.S.C. 1681u(k), 50 U.S.C. 3162(c).

[28] 15 U.S.C. 1681u(d); 50 U.S.C. 3162(b).

[29] 15 U.S.C. 1681u(c).

[30] P.L. 107-56, §505, 115 Stat. 365-66 (2001).

[31] "The information acquired through NSLs is extremely valuable to national security investigations.... Unfortunately, however, NSLs were of limited utility prior to the PATRIOT Act. While records held by third parties may generally be subpoenaed by a grand jury in a criminal investigation so long as those records are relevant, the standard for obtaining such records through an NSL was much higher before October of 2001.
"The FBI had to have specific and articulable facts that the information requested pertained to a foreign power or an (continued...)

Subsection 358(g) of the USA PATRIOT Act amended the Fair Credit Reporting Act to add a fifth and final NSL section; the provision had one particularly noteworthy feature, it was available not merely to the FBI but to any government agency investigating or analyzing international terrorism:

> Notwithstanding section 1681b of this title or any other provision of this subchapter, a consumer reporting agency shall furnish a consumer report of a consumer and all other information in a consumer's file to a government agency authorized to conduct investigations of, or intelligence or counterintelligence activities or analysis related to, international terrorism when presented with a written certification by such government agency that such information is necessary for the agency's conduct or such investigation, activity or analysis.[32]

Although the subsection's legislative history treats it as a matter of first impression,[33] Congress's obvious intent was to provide other agencies with the national security letter authority comparable to that enjoyed by the FBI under the Fair Credit Reporting Act. The new section had a nondisclosure and a safe harbor subsection, 15 U.S.C. 1681v(c), (e), but no express means of judicial enforcement or penalties for improper disclosure of a request under the section.

In the 108th Congress, the scope of the Right to Financial Privacy Act NSL was enlarged by defining the financial institutions subject to the authority to include not only banks and credit unions but also car dealers, jewelers, and real estate agents, among others.[34] The same Congress

---

(...continued)
agent of a foreign power. This requirement often prohibited the FBI from using NSLs to develop evidence at the early stage of an investigation, which is precisely when they are the most useful.
"The prior standard, Mr. Chairman, put the cart before the horse. Agents trying to determine whether or not there were specific and articulable facts that a certain individual was a terrorist or spy were precluded from using an NSL in this inquiry because, in order to use an NSL, they first had to be in possession of such facts.
"Suppose, for example, investigators were tracking a known al-Qaeda operative and saw him having lunch with three individuals. A responsible agent would want to conduct a preliminary investigation of those individuals and find out, among other things, with whom they had recently been in communication.
"Before the passage of the PATRIOT Act, however, the FBI could not have issued an NSL to obtain such information. While investigators could have demonstrated that this information was relevant to an ongoing terrorism investigation, they could not have demonstrated sufficient specific, and articulable facts that the individuals in question were agents of a foreign power," *Material Witness Provisions of the Criminal Code, and the Implementation of the USA PATRIOT Act: Section 505 That Addresses National Security Letters, and Section 804 That Addresses Jurisdiction Over Crimes Committed at U.S. Facilities Abroad: Hearing Before the Subcomm. on Crime, Terrorism, and Homeland Security of the House Comm. on the Judiciary*, 109th Cong., 1st Sess. at 9-10 (2005) (testimony of Matthew Berry, Office of Legal Policy, U.S. Department of Justice).

[32] P.L. 107-56, §358(g), 115 Stat. 327 (2001).

[33] E.g., H.Rept. 107-250, at 60-1 ("This section facilitates government access to information contained in suspected terrorists' credit reports when the government inquiry relates to an investigation, of or intelligence activity or analysis relating to, domestic or international terrorism. Even though private entities such as lender and insurers can access an individual's credit history, the government is strictly limited in its ability under current law to obtain the information. This section would permit those investigating suspected terrorists prompt access to credit histories that may reveal key information about the terrorist's plan or source of refunding—without notifying the target").

[34] P.L. 108-177, §374, 117 Stat. 2628 (2004), 12 U.S.C. 3414(d), adopts the definition of financial institution found in 31 U.S.C. 5312(a)(2), (c)(1), that is: "(A) an insured bank (as defined in 12 U.S.C. 1813(h)); (B) a commercial bank or trust company; (C) a private banker; (D) an agency or branch of a foreign bank in the United States; (E) any credit union; (F) a thrift institution; (G) a broker or dealer registered with the Securities and Exchange Commission; (H) a broker or dealer in securities or commodities; (I) an investment banker or investment company; (J) a currency exchange; (K) an issuer, redeemer, or cashier of travelers' checks, checks, money orders, or similar instruments; (L) an operator of a credit card system; (M) an insurance company; (N) a dealer in precious metals, stones, or jewels; (O) a pawnbroker; (P) a loan or finance company; (Q) a travel agency; (R) a licensed sender of money or any other person (continued...)

---

saw a number of proposals introduced to exempt libraries from the reach of the communications NSL,[35] to increase congressional oversight over the use of NSL authority,[36] and to add the USA PATRIOT Act section 505 NSL amendments to the list of those temporary sections scheduled to expire on December 31, 2005.[37] The 108th also witnessed the introduction of proposals that ultimately evolved into the NSL amendments in the USA PATRIOT Improvement and Reauthorization Act. H.R. 3179, introduced by Representative Sensenbrenner. They would have reinforced the five national security letter provisions with explicit authority for judicial enforcement[38] and with criminal penalties for improper disclosure of the issuance of such letters. The penalties were to be the same as those proposed under the general administrative subpoena bills offered in the 108th—imprisonment for not more than five years when committed with the intent to obstruct and for not more than one year otherwise, proposed 18 U.S.C. 1510(e). A Justice Department witness explained that, "Oftentimes, the premature disclosure of an ongoing terrorism investigation can lead to a host of negative repercussions, including the destruction of evidence, the flight of suspected terrorists, and the frustration of efforts to identify additional terrorist conspirators. For these reasons, the FBI has forgone using NSLs in some investigations for fear that the recipients of those NSLs would compromise an investigation by disclosing the fact that they had been sent an NSL."[39] The enforcement provision would have been backed by the court's contempt power, proposed 18 U.S.C. 2332h.[40] It had no explicit provisions, however, to permit the recipient to file a motion to quash or modify the NSL request.

(...continued)

who engages as a business in the transmission of funds, including any person who engages as a business in an informal money transfer system or any network of people who engage as a business in facilitating the transfer of money domestically or internationally outside of the conventional financial institutions system; (S) a telegraph company; (T) a business engaged in vehicle sales, including automobile, airplane, and boat sales; (U) persons involved in real estate closings and settlements; (V) the United States Postal Service; (W) an agency of the United States Government or of a State or local government carrying out a duty or power of a business described in this paragraph; (X) a casino, gambling casino, or gaming establishment with an annual gaming revenue of more than $1,000,000 which—(i) is licensed as a casino, gambling casino, or gaming establishment under the laws of any State or any political subdivision of any State; or (ii) is an Indian gaming operation conducted under or pursuant to the Indian Gaming Regulatory Act other than an operation which is limited to class I gaming (as defined in section 4(6) of such Act); (Y) any business or agency which engages in any activity which the Secretary of the Treasury determines, by regulation, to be an activity which is similar to, related to, or a substitute for any activity in which any business described in this paragraph is authorized to engage; (Z) any other business designated by the Secretary whose cash transactions have a high degree of usefulness in criminal, tax, or regulatory matters; [or (AA)] any futures commission merchant, commodity trading advisor, or commodity pool operator registered, or required to register, under the Commodity Exchange Act."

[35] H.R. 3352, §5 (Rep. Otter); S. 1158, §3 (Sen. Boxer); S. 1507, §2 (Sen. Feingold); S. 1552, §4(b) (Sen. Murkowski); and S. 1709, §5 (Sen. Craig).

[36] S. 436, §3 (Sen. Leahy).

[37] H.R. 3171, §4 (Rep. Kucinich); H.R. 3352, §7 (Rep. Otter); S. 1695, §2 (Sen. Leahy); and S. 1709, §6 (Sen. Craig).

[38] In *Doe v. Ashcroft*, 334 F.Supp.2d 471, 496-501 (S.D.N.Y. 2004), the Government argued unsuccessfully that the NSL statutes should be understood to include an implicit judicial enforcement component.

[39] *Anti-Terrorism Intelligence Tools Improvement Act of 2003: Hearing Before the Subcomm. on Crime, Terrorism, and Homeland Security (House Hearing)*, 108th Cong., 2nd Sess., 7-8 (2004)(prepared statement of United States Assistant Attorney General Daniel J. Bryant).

[40] Proposed 18 U.S.C. 2332h ("In the case of a refusal to comply with a request for records, a report, or other information made to any person under section 2709(b) of this title, section 625 (a) or (b) or 626 of the Fair Credit Reporting Act [15 U.S.C. 1681u, 1681v], section 1114(a)(5)A) of the right to Financial Privacy Act [12 U.S.C. 3414, or section 802(a) of the National Security Act of 1947 [50 U.S.C. 3162(a)], the Attorney General may invoke the aid of any court of the United States within the jurisdiction of which the investigation is carried on or the person resides, carries on business, or may be found, to compel compliance with the request. The court may issue an order requiring the person to comply with the request. Any failure to obey the order of the court may be punished by the court as contempt thereof. Any process under this section may be served in any judicial district in which the person may be (continued...)

Pre-amendment Judicial Action

Proponents of legislative proposals in the 108th Congress did not enjoy the benefit of two court decisions that colored the debate over NSL authority during the 109th Congress. *Doe v. Ashcroft,*[41] reached much the same conclusion on the First Amendment issue: narrowly defined, the government's and *Doe v. Gonzales*[42] suggested that the NSL statutes could not withstand constitutional scrutiny unless more explicit provisions were made for judicial review and permissible disclosure by recipients. In essence, *Doe v. Ashcroft* found that the language of 18 U.S.C. 2709 and the practices surrounding its use offended (1) the Fourth Amendment because "in all but the exceptional case it [had] the effect of authorizing coercive searches effectively immune from any judicial process," 334 F.Supp.2d at 506, and (2) the First Amendment because its sweeping, permanent secrecy order feature applied "in every case, to every person, in perpetuity, with no vehicle for the ban to ever be lifted from the recipient or other persons affected under any circumstances, either by the FBI itself, or pursuant to judicial process," *id.* at 476.

NSL Amendments in the 109th Congress

Both USA PATRIOT Act reauthorization statutes—P.L. 109-177 (H.R. 3199) and P.L. 109-178 (S. 2271)[43]—amended each of the NSL statutes. They

- created a judicial enforcement mechanism and a judicial review procedure for both the requests and accompanying nondisclosure requirements;[44]

- established specific penalties for failure to comply or to observe the nondisclosure requirements;[45]

- made it clear that the nondisclosure requirements did not preclude a recipient from consulting an attorney;[46]

- provided a process to ease the nondisclosure requirement;[47]

- expanded congressional oversight;[48]

- called for an Inspector General's audit of use of the authority.[49]

(...continued)
found").

[41] 334 F.Supp.2d 471 (S.D.N.Y. 2004), vac'd and remanded, 449 F.3d 415 (2d Cir. 2006), after remand, 500 F.Supp.2d 379 (S.D.N.Y. 2007), aff'd in part, rev'd in part and remanded, 549 F.3d 861 (2d Cir. 2008), after remand, 665 F.Supp.2d 426 (S..D.N.Y. 2009); see also, *Doe v. Holder*, 703 F.Supp.2d. 313 (S.D.N.Y. 2010).

[42] 386 F.Supp.2d 66 (D.Conn. 2005), dism'd as moot, 449 F.3d 415 (2d Cir. 2006).

[43] 120 Stat. 192 (2006) and 120 Stat. 278 (2006), respectively.

[44] 28 U.S.C. 3511.

[45] 28 U.S.C. 3511(c), 18 U.S.C. 1510(e).

[46] 12 U.S.C. 3414((a)(3)(A); 15 U.S.C. 1681v(c)(1), 1681u(d)(1); 18 U.S.C. 2709(c)(1); 50 U.S.C.3162(b)(1).

[47] 28 U.S.C. 3511(b).

[48] P.L. 109-177, §118.

[49] P.L. 109-177, §119.

Post-Amendment NSL Attributes

Addressees and Certifying Officials

The five NSL statutes share a number of common attributes, although each has its own individual features as well. They are most distinctive with respect to the nature of the businesses to whom they may be addressed. The Electronic Communication Privacy Act NSLs are addressed to communications providers.[50] Those issued under the authority of the Right to Financial Privacy Act may be directed to any financial institution, which as noted earlier, includes not only banks and credit unions, but credit card companies, car dealers, jewelers and a number of entities that are likely the scene of large cash transactions.[51] The Fair Credit Reporting Act NSLs may be addressed to consumer credit reporting agencies.[52] Recipients of the National Security Act NSLs may include either financial institutions or consumer credit reporting agencies as well as any commercial entity with information concerning an agency employee's travel.[53]

FBI officials are authorized to provide the initial certification required for issuance of an NSL under any of the five statutes. In three instances, the authority is exclusive; in the other two, it is enjoyed by other federal officials as well. In the case of the Electronic Communications Privacy Act NSL section, the Right to Financial Privacy Act section, and one of the Fair Credit Report Act NSL sections, issuance requires the certification of either the Director of the FBI, a senior FBI official (no lower than the Deputy Assistant Director), or the Special Agent in Charge of an FBI field office.[54]

Certifying officials under the other statutes are described more broadly. The National Security Act NSL section contemplates certification by officials from a wider range of agencies; the second Fair Credit Reporting Act NSL section allows certification by both a wider range of agencies and a wider range of officials. Senior officials no lower than Assistant Secretary or Assistant Director of an agency whose employee with access to classified material is under investigation may certify a National Security Act NSL request.[55] A designated supervisory official of any agency "authorized to conduct investigations of, or intelligence or counterintelligence activities and analysis related to, international terrorism" may certify a NSL request under the second, more recent Fair Credit Reporting Act section.[56]

Purpose, Standards, Information Covered

Although variously phrased, the purpose for each of the NSLs is to acquire information related to the requesting agency's national security concerns. The most common statement of purpose is "to protect against international terrorism or clandestine intelligence activities."[57] The more recent of

---

[50] 18 U.S.C. 2709.

[51] 12 U.S.C. 3414(a), (d).

[52] 15 U.S.C. 1681u(a), 1681v(a).

[53] 50 U.S.C. 3162(a).

[54] 18 U.S.C. 2709 (b); 12 U.S.C. 3414(a)(5)(A); 15 U.S.C. 1681u(b).

[55] 50 U.S.C. 3162(a)(3).

[56] 15 U.S.C. 1681v(a).

[57] 18 U.S.C. 2709(b); 12 U.S.C. 3414(a)(5)(A); 15 U.S.C. 1681u(b).

the Fair Credit Reporting Act NSL sections simply indicates that the information must be sought for the requesting intelligence agency's investigation, activity or analysis.[58] The National Security Act NSL authority is available to conduct law enforcement investigations, counterintelligence inquiries, and security determinations.[59] As to standards, the Electronic Communications Privacy Act authorizes NSLs for relevant information.[60] The same standard may apply to the others which are a little more cryptic, authorizing NSLs when the information is "sought for"[61] or "is necessary"[62] for the statutory purpose.

The communications NSL provision and the earlier of the two credit agency NSL statutes are fairly specific in their descriptions of the information that may be requested through an NSL. An Electronic Communications Privacy Act NSL may request a customer's name, address, length of service and billing records.[63] The older of the two Fair Credit Report Act sections authorizes a NSL to acquire name, address or former address, place or former place of employment, and the name and address of any financial institution with which the consumer has or once had an account.[64] The Right to Financial Privacy Act NSL provision covers the financial records of a financial institution's customers;[65] the second and more recent Fair Credit Reporting Act NSL provision covers a consumer reporting agency's consumer reports and "all other" consumer information in its files.[66] The National Security Act provision is at once the most inclusive and the most restricted. It authorizes NSLs for financial information and records and consumer reports held by any financial agency, institution, holding company or consumer reporting agency, and for travel information held by any commercial entity.[67] On the other hand, it is the only provision that limits the information provided to that pertaining to the target of the agency's investigation and to information of a kind whose disclosure the target has previously approved.[68]

Confidentiality

Prior to their amendment in the 109th Congress, the NSL statutes generally featured an open ended confidentiality clause. The communications NSL provision for example declared, "No wire or electronic communication service provider, or officer, or employee, or agent thereof, shall disclose to any person that the Federal Bureau of Investigation has sought or obtained access to information or records under this section."[69] The statutes did not indicate whether a recipient might consult an attorney in order to ascertain his rights and obligations, nor whether it might ever be lifted. It was this silence in the face of a seemingly absolute, permanent nondisclosure

---

[58] 15 U.S.C. 1681v(a).

[59] 50 U.S.C. 3162(a)(1).

[60] 18 U.S.C. 2709(b).

[61] 15 U.S.C. 1681u(a); 12 U.S.C. 3414(a)(5)(A).

[62] 15 U.S.C. 1681v; 50 U.S.C. 3162(a).

[63] 18 U.S.C. 2709(b).

[64] 15 U.S.C. 1681u(a),(b).

[65] 12 U.S.C. 3414(a)(5)(A).

[66] 15 U.S.C. 1681v(a)

[67] 50 U.S.C. 3162(a)(1).

[68] 50 U.S.C. 3162(a)(2),(3).

[69] 18 U.S.C. 2709(c) (2000 ed.); see also, 12 U.S.C. 3414(a)(5)(D) (2000 ed.); 15 U.S.C. 1681u(d) (2000 ed.); 15 U.S.C. 1681v(c) (2002 Supp.); 50 U.S.C. 436(b) (2000 ed.).

command that the early *Doe* courts found constitutionally unacceptable[70] and that perhaps led to the reconstruction of the NSL confidentiality requirements in their current form.

As NSL statutes now read, secrecy is not absolutely required. Instead NSL recipients are bound to secrecy only upon the certification of the requesting agency that disclosure of the request or response may result in a danger to national security; may interfere with diplomatic relations or with a criminal, counterterrorism, or counterintelligence investigation; or may endanger the physical safety of an individual. A recipient may disclose the request to those necessary to comply with the request and to an attorney the recipient consults for related legal advice or assistance. In doing so, the recipient must advise them of the secrecy requirements. Aside from its attorney and at the agency's election, the recipient must also identify those to whom it has disclosed the request. A recipient may petition the court to modify or extinguish any NSL secrecy requirement within a year of issuance.[71] Thereafter, it may petition to have the veil of secrecy lifted, although it may resubmit a rejected request only once a year.[72] In all instances, section 3511 declares conclusive and warranting continued secrecy the certification by certain officials that disclosure might create a danger to national security, interfere with diplomatic relations or ongoing investigations, or jeopardize personal safety.[73] A breach of a confidentiality requirement committed knowingly and with the intent to obstruct an investigation or related judicial proceedings is punishable by imprisonment for not more than five years and/or a fine of not more than $250,000 (not more than $500,000 for an organization).[74]

Judicial Review and Enforcement

In addition to authority to review and set aside NSL nondisclosure requirements, the federal courts also enjoy jurisdiction to review and enforce the underlying NSL requests. Recipients may petition and be granted an order modifying or setting aside an NSL, if the court finds that compliance would be unreasonable, oppressive, or otherwise unlawful.[75] Subpoenas issued under the Federal Rules of Criminal Procedure may be modified or quashed if compliance would be unreasonable or oppressive.[76] The Rule affords protection against undue burdens and protects privileged communications.[77] Compliance with a particular NSL might be unduly burdensome in some situations, but the circumstances under which NSLs are used suggest few federally recognized privileges. The Rule also imposes a relevancy requirement, but in the context of an investigation a motion to quash will be denied unless it can be shown that "there is no reasonable possibility that the category of materials the Government seeks will produce information relevant" to the investigation.[78] The authority to modify or set aside a NSL that is unlawful

---

[70] *Doe v. Ashcroft*, 334 F.Supp.2d 471, 522 (S.D.N.Y. 2004). and *Doe v. Gonzales*, 386 F.Supp.2d 66, 78-81 (D.Conn. 2005).

[71] 28 U.S.C. 3511(b)(2). As construed by the Second Circuit, the government is obliged to advise a recipient that the recipient has a period of time within which to decide if he would like the government to seek judicial review of its determination of the need for secrecy, *John Doe, Inc. v. Mukasey*, 549 F.3d 861, 883 (2d Cir. 2008).

[72] 28 U.S.C. 3511(b)(3).

[73] 28 U.S.C. 3511(b)(2), (3). The Second Circuit has declared this component of the procedure unconstitutional, *John Doe, Inc. v. Mukasey*, 549 F.3d at 883.

[74] 18 U.S.C. 1510(e), 3571, 3559.

[75] 28 U.S.C. 3511.

[76] F.R.Crim.P. 17(c)(2).

[77] 2 WRIGHT, FEDERAL PRACTICE AND PROCEDURE §275 (Crim. 3d ed. 2000).

[78] *United States v. R. Enterprises, Inc.*, 498 U.S. 292, 301 (1991).

affords the court an opportunity to determine whether the NSL in question complies with the statutory provisions under which it was issued. On the other hand, the court's authority may be invoked to enforce the NSL against a recalcitrant recipient and failure to comply thereafter is punishable as contempt of court.[79]

Dissemination

Attorney General's guidelines govern the sharing of information acquired in response to NSLs under two statutes.[80] A third, the older of the two Fair Credit Report Act sections, limits dissemination to sharing within the FBI, with other agencies to the extent necessary to secure approval of a foreign counterintelligence investigation, or with military investigators when the information concerns a member of the Armed Forces.[81] The National Security Act authorizes dissemination of NSL information to the agency of the employee under investigation, to the Justice Department for law enforcement or counterintelligence purposes, or to another federal agency if the information is clearly relevant to its mission.[82] The more recent Fair Credit Reporting Act NSL section has no explicit provision on restricting dissemination.[83]

Liability, Fees and Oversight

Since judicial enforcement is a feature new to all but one of the NSL statutes,[84] they might be expected to include other incentives to overcome recipient resistance. Three do offer immunity from civil liability for recipients who comply in good faith,[85] and two offer fees or reimbursement to defer the costs of compliance.[86]

The confidentiality that necessarily surrounds NSL requests could give rise to concerns of governmental overreaching. Consequently, regular reports on the use of NSL authority must be made to the congressional intelligence and judiciary committees and in some instances to the banking committees.[87] Moreover, section 119 of the USA PATRIOT Improvement and Reauthorization Act instructs the Inspector General of the Department of Justice to audit and to report to the judiciary and intelligence committees as to the Department's use of the authority in the years following expansion of the authority in the USA PATRIOT Act. The section also directs

---

[79] 28 U.S.C. 3511(c).

[80] 12 U.S.C. 3414(a)(5)(B)("The Federal Bureau of Investigation may disseminate information obtained pursuant to this paragraph only as provided in guidelines approved by the Attorney General for foreign intelligence collection and foreign counterintelligence investigations conducted by the Federal Bureau of Investigation, and, with respect to dissemination to an agency of the United States, only if such information is clearly relevant to the authorized responsibilities of such agency"); see also, 18 U.S.C. 2709(d).

[81] 15 U.S.C. 1681u(f).

[82] 50 U.S.C. 3162(e).

[83] 15 U.S.C. 1681v.

[84] In addition to the newly added judicial enforcement mechanism in 28 U.S.C. 3511, the earlier Fair Credit Report Act NSL sections had a limited judicial enforcement subsection, as it had for some time, 15 U.S.C. 1681u(c).

[85] 15 U.S.C. 1681u(k), 1681v(e); 50 U.S.C. 3162(c)(2).

[86] 15 U.S.C. 1681u(e); 50 U.S.C. 3162(d).

[87] P.L. 109-177, §118(a)(adding the judiciary committees as recipients of all NSL required reports); 12 U.S.C. 3414(a)(5)(C)(intelligence committees); 18 U.S.C. 2709 (intelligence and judiciary committees); 15 U.S.C. 1681u(h)(intelligence and banking committees), 1681v(judiciary, intelligence, and banking committees).

the Attorney General and the Director of National Intelligence to report to Congress on the feasibility of establishing minimization requirements for the NSLs.

The chart that follows summarizes the differences among the five NSL sections:

Table 1. Profile of the Current NSL Statutes

NSL statute	18 U.S.C. 2709	12 U.S.C. 3414	15 U.S.C. 1681u	15 U.S.C. 1681v	50 U.S.C. 3162
Addressee	communications providers	financial institutions	consumer credit agencies	consumer credit agencies	financial institutions, consumer credit agencies, travel agencies
Certifying officials	senior FBI officials and SACs	senior FBI officials and SACs	senior FBI officials and SACs	supervisory official of an agency investigating, conducting intelligence activities relating to or analyzing int'l terrorism	senior officials no lower than Ass't Secretary or Ass't Director of agency w/ employees w/ access to classified material
Information covered	identified customer's name, address, length of service, and billing info	identified customer financial records	identified consumer's name, address, former address, place and former place of employment	all information relating to an identified consumer	all financial information relating to consenting, identified employee
Standard/ Purpose	relevant to an investigation to protect against int'l terrorism or clandestine intelligence activities	sought for foreign counter-intelligence purposes to protect against int'l terrorism or clandestine intelligence activities	sought for an investigation to protect against int'l terrorism or clandestine intelligence activities	necessary for the agency's investigation, activities, or analysis relating to int'l terrorism	necessary to conduct a law enforcement investigation, counter-intelligence inquiry or security determination
Dissemination	only per Att'y Gen. guidelines	only per Att'y Gen. guidelines	w/i FBI, to secure approval for intell. investigation, to military investigators when inform. relates to military member	no statutory provision	only to agency of employee under investigation, DOJ for law enforcement or intell. purposes, or fed. agency when clearly relevant to mission
Immunity/fees	no provisions	no provisions	fees; immunity for good faith compliance with a NSL	immunity for good faith compliance with a NSL	reimbursement; immunity for good faith compliance with a NSL

Source: Congressional Research Service, based on the statutes cited in the table.

Inspector General's Reports

The First IG Report

The Department of Justice Inspector General reports, one released in March of 2007, the second in March of 2008, and the third in January of 2010, were less than totally favorable.[88] The first report noted that FBI use of NSLs had increased dramatically, expanding from 8,500 requests in 2000 to 47,000 in 2005, *IG Report I* at 120. During the three years under review, the percentage of NSLs used to investigate Americans ("U.S. persons") increased from 39% in 2003 to 53% in 2005.[89] A substantial majority of the requests involved records relating to telephone or e-mail communications, *id.*

The report and the subsequent report a year later provided a glimpse at how the individual NSL statutes were used and why they were considered available. In case of the 18 U.S.C. 2709, the Electronic Communications Privacy Act (ECPA) NSL statute, the reports explained that:

> Through national security letters, an FBI field office obtained telephone toll billing records and subscriber information about an investigative subject in a counterterrorism case. The information obtained identified the various telephone numbers with which the subject had frequent contact. Analysis of the telephone records enabled the FBI to identify a group of individuals residing in the same vicinity as the subject. The FBI initiated investigations on these individuals to determine if there was a terrorist cell operating in the city.[90]

> Headquarters and field personnel told us that the principal objective of the most frequently used type of NSL—ECPA NSLs seeking telephone toll billing records, electronic communication transactional records, or subscriber information (telephone and e-mail)—is to develop evidence to support applications for FISA orders.[91]

The Right to Financial Privacy Act (RFPA) NSL statute, 12 U.S.C. 3414(a)(5), also affords authorities access a wide range of information (bank transaction records v. telephone transaction records) as demonstrated by the instances where it proved useful:

> The FBI conducted a multi-jurisdictional counterterrorism investigation of convenience store owners in the United States who allegedly sent funds to known Hawaladars (persons who use the Hawala money transfer system in lieu of or parallel to traditional banks) in the Middle

---

[88] U.S. Department of Justice, Office of the Inspector General, *A Review of the Federal Bureau of Investigation's Use of National Security Letters* (*IG Report I*) (March 2007); *A Review of the FBI's Use of National Security Letters: Assessment of Corrective Actions and Examination of NSL Usage in 2006* (*IG Report II*) (March 2008); *A Review of the Federal Bureau of Investigation's Use of Exigent Letters and Other Informal Requests for Telephone Records* (*IG Report III*), all three available at http://www.usdoj.gov/oig/special/index htm.

[89] *Id.* A "U.S. person" is generally understood to mean "a citizen of the United States, an alien lawfully admitted for permanent residence (as defined in section 1101(a)(2) of title 8), an unincorporated association a substantial number of members of which are citizens of the United States or aliens lawfully admitted for permanent residence, or a corporation which is incorporated in the United States, but does not include a corporation or an association which is a foreign power, as defined in subsection(a)(1), (2), or (3) of this section," 50 U.S.C. 1801.

[90] *IG Report I* at 49.

[91] *IG Report II* at 65. The Foreign Intelligence Surveillance Act (FISA) authorizes the FBI to apply for court orders in national security cases authorizing electronic surveillance, physical searches, the installation and use of pen registers and trap and trace devices, and access to business records and other tangible property, 50 U.S.C. 1801-1862.

East. The funds were transferred to suspected Al Qaeda affiliates. The possible violations committed by the subjects of these cases included money laundering, sale of untaxed cigarettes, check cashing fraud, illegal sale of pseudoephedrine (the precursor ingredient used to manufacture methamphetamine), unemployment insurance fraud, welfare fraud, immigration fraud, income tax violations, and sale of counterfeit merchandise. [92]

The FBI issued national security letters for the convenience store owners' bank account records. The records showed that two persons received millions of dollars from the subjects and that another subject had forwarded large sums of money to one of these individuals. The bank analysis identified sources and recipients of the money transfers and assisted in the collection of information on targets of the investigation overseas. [93]

The Fair Credit Reporting Act NSL statutes, 15 U.S.C. 1681u (FCRAu) and 1681v (FCRAv) can be even more illuminating, "The supervisor of a counterterrorism squad told us that the FCRA NSLs enable the FBI to see 'how their investigative subjects conduct their day-to-day activities, how they get their money, and whether they are engaged in white collar crime that could be relevant to their investigations.'"[94]

Overall, the report notes that the FBI used the information gleaned from NSLs for a variety of purposes, "to determine if further investigation is warranted; to generate leads for other field offices, Joint Terrorism Task Forces, or other federal agencies; and to corroborate information developed from other investigative techniques."[95] Moreover, information supplied in response to NSLs provides the grist of FBI analytical intelligence reports and various FBI databases.[96]

The report was somewhat critical, however, of the FBI's initial performance:

> [W]e found that the FBI used NSLs in violation of applicable NSL statutes, Attorney General Guidelines, and internal FBI policies. In addition, we found that the FBI circumvented the requirements of the ECPA NSL statute when it issued at least 739 "exigent letters" to obtain telephone toll billing records and subscriber information from three telephone companies without first issuing NSLs. Moreover, in a few other instances, the FBI sought or obtained telephone toll billing records in the absence of a national security investigation, when it sought and obtained consumer full credit reports in a counterintelligence investigation, and when it sought and obtained financial records and telephone toll billing records without first issuing NSLs. *Id.* at 124.

More specifically, the report found that:

- a "significant number of NSL-related possible violations were not being identified or reported" as required;

- the only FBI data collection system produced "inaccurate" results;

- the FBI issued over 700 exigent letters acquiring information in a manner that "circumvented the ECPA NSL statute and violated the Attorney General's Guidelines ... and internal FBI policy;"

---

[92] Critics might suggest that these offenses are "possible" in the operation of any convenience store.

[93] *IG Report I* at 50.

[94] *Id.* at 51.

[95] *Id.* at 65.

[96] Id.

- the FBI's Counterterrorism Division initiated over 300 NSLs in a manner that precluded effective review prior to approval;

- 60% of the individual files examined showed violations of FBI internal control policies;

- the FBI did not retain signed copies of the NSLs it issued;

- the FBI had not provided clear guidance on the application of the Attorney General's least-intrusive-feasible-investigative-technique standard in the case of NSLs;

- the precise interpretation of toll billing information as it appears in the ECPA NSL statute is unclear;

- SAC supervision of the attorneys responsible for review of the legal adequacy of proposed NSLs made some of the attorneys reluctant to question the adequacy of the underlying investigation previously approved by the SAC;

- there was no indication that the FBI's misuse of NSL authority constituted criminal conduct;

- personnel both at FBI headquarters and in the field considered NSL use indispensable; and

- information generated by NSLs was fed into a number of FBI systems. *IG Report I* at 121-24.

Exigent Letters

Prior to enactment of the Electronic Communications Privacy Act (ECPA), the Supreme Court held that customers had no Fourth Amendment protected privacy rights in the records the telephone company maintained relating to their telephone use.[97] Where a recognized expectation of privacy exists for Fourth Amendment purposes, the Amendment's usual demands such as those of probable cause, particularity, and a warrant may be eased in the face of exigent circumstances. For example, the Fourth Amendment requirement that officers must knock and announce their purpose before forcibly entering a building to execute a warrant can be eased in the presence of certain exigent circumstances such as the threat of the destruction of evidence or danger to the officers.[98] Satisfying Fourth Amendment requirements, however, does not necessarily satisfy statutory prohibitions.

The ECPA prohibits communications service providers from supplying information concerning customer records unless one of the statutory exceptions applies.[99] There are specific exceptions for disclosure upon receipt of a grand jury subpoena[100] or an NSL.[101] A service provider who

---

[97] *Smith v. Maryland*, 442 U.S. 735, 745 (1979)

[98] *Richards v. Wisconsin*, 520 U.S. 385, 391 (1997); *Wilson v. Arkansas*, 514 U.S. 927, 936 (1995).

[99] 18 U.S.C. 2702(c).

[100] 18 U.S.C. 2703(c)(2).

[101] 18 U.S.C. 2709(a).

knowingly or intentionally violates the prohibition is subject to civil liability,[102] but there are no criminal penalties for the breach.

The Inspector General found that contrary to assertions that "the FBI would obtain telephone records only after it served NSLs or grand jury subpoenas, the FBI obtained telephone bill records and subscriber information prior to serving NSLs or grand jury subpoenas" by using "exigent letters."[103] The FBI responded that it had barred the use of exigent letters, but emphasized that the term "exigent letter" does not include emergency disclosures under the exception now found in 18 U.S.C. 2702(c)(4). Thus, the FBI might request that a service provider invoke that exception to the record disclosure bar "if the provider reasonably believes that an emergency involving immediate danger of death or serious physical injury to any person justifies disclosure of the information," 18 U.S.C. 2702(c)(4). Moreover, the Justice Department's Office of Legal Counsel subsequently advised the FBI in a classified memorandum that "under certain circumstances the ECPA does not prohibit electronic communications service providers from disclosing certain call detail records to the FBI on a voluntary basis without legal process or a qualifying emergency under Section 2702."[104]

The Second IG Report

The second IG Report reviewed the FBI's use of national security letter authority during calendar year 2006 and the corrective measures taken following the issuance of the IG's first report. The second Report concluded that:

- "the FBI's use of national security letters in 2006 continued the upward trend ... identified ... for the period covering 2003 through 2005;

- "the percentage of NSL requests generated from investigations of U.S. persons continued to increase significantly, from approximately 39% of all NSL requests issued in 2003 to approximately 57% of all NSL requests issued in 2006;"

- the FBI and DOJ are committed to correcting the problems identified in *IG Report I* and "have made significant progress in addressing the need to improve compliance in the FBI's use of NSLs;" [and]

- "it [was] too early to definitively state whether the new systems and controls developed by the FBI and the Department will eliminate fully the problems with NSLs that we identified," *IG Report II* at 8-9.

The Third IG Report

The third IG Report examined the FBI's use of exigent letters and other informal means of acquiring communication service provider's customer records in lieu of relying on NSL authority

---

[102] 18 U.S.C. 2707(a).

[103] *IG Report I* at 90.

[104] *Report by the Office of the Inspector General of the Department of Justice on the Federal Bureau of Investigation's Use of Exigent Letters and Other Informal Requests for Telephone Records: Hearing Before the Subcomm. on the Constitution, Civil Rights, and Civil Liberties of the House Comm. on the Judiciary*, 111th Cong. 2d sess. 22 (2010) (*2010 Hearings*) (statement of Department of Justice Inspector General Glenn Fine) (referring to a January, 2010 OLC memorandum).

during the period from 2003 to 2007.[105] The IG's Office discovered that "the FBI's use exigent letters became so casual, routine, and unsupervised that employees of all three communications service providers sometimes generated exigent letters for FBI personnel to sign and return to them."[106]

Some of the informality was apparently the product of proximity. In order to facilitate cooperation, communications providers had assigned employees to FBI offices. In addition to a relaxed exigent letter process, the on-site feature gave rise to a practice of sneak peeks, that is, of providing the FBI with "a preview of the available information for a targeted phone number, without documentation of any justification for the request."[107] "In fact, at times the service providers' employees simply invited FBI personnel to view the telephone records on their computer screens. One senior FBI counterterrorism official described the culture of casual requests for telephone records by observing, 'It [was] like having the ATM in your living room."[108]

Not surprisingly, the IG's review " ... found widespread use by the FBI of exigent letters and other informal requests for telephone records. These other requests were made ... without first providing legal process or even exigent letters. The FBI also obtained telephone records through improper 'sneak peeks,' community of interest ███, and hot-number ███ Many of these practices violated FBI guidelines, Department policy, and the ECPA statute. In addition, we found that the FBI also made inaccurate statements to the FISA Court related to its use of exigent letters."[109]

Although critical of the FBI's initial response and recommending further steps to prevent reoccurrence, the IG's Report concluded that "the FBI took appropriate action to stop the use of exigent letters and to address the problems created by their use."[110]

Post-Amendment Judicial Action

Following the 2006 USA PATRIOT Act amendments, the District Court for the Southern District of New York revisited the issue anew and concluded that the revised NSL procedures violated both First Amendment and separation of powers principles.[111] It enjoined Justice Department officials from issuing NSLs under Section 2709 or from enforcing compliance with existing orders.[112] However, it stayed the order pending appeal.[113] The Court of Appeals was similarly disposed, but concluded that the government could invoke the secrecy and judicial review

---

[105] *IG Report III* at 1.

[106] *2010 Hearings* at 14 (statement of Department of Justice Inspector General Glenn Fine)

[107] *Id.* at 15.

[108] *Id.*

[109] *Id.* at 288 (redaction in the original).

[110] *IG Report III* at 289.

[111] *Doe v. Gonzalez*, 500 F.Supp.2d 379 (S.D.N.Y. 2007), aff'd in part, rev'd in part, and remanded, sub nom., *John Doe, Inc. v. Mukasey*, 549 F.861 (2d Cir. 2008).

[112] *Doe v. Gonzalez* 500 F.Supp.2d at 425-26.

[113] *Id.* at 426.

authority of the 18 U.S.C. 2709 and 18 U.S.C. 3511 in a limited but constitutionally permissible manner.[114]

The issues before the Court of Appeals were (1) whether the nondisclosure features of section 2709(c) should be subject to First Amendment strict scrutiny and (2) whether judicial review subject to the conclusive weight of an executive branch certification under section 3511 posed constitutional concerns.

The pre-amendment *Doe* cases had concluded that section 2709(c), which then broadly prohibited disclosure of receipt of an NSL, "work[ed] as both a prior restraint on speech and a content-based restriction, and hence, [was] subject to strict scrutiny."[115] "Under strict scrutiny review," the Supreme Court has explained, "the Government must demonstrate that the nondisclosure requirement is narrowly tailored to promote a compelling Government interest."[116] Moreover, there can be "no less restrictive alternatives that would be at least as effective in achieving the legitimate purpose that the statute was enacted to serve."[117] When a suspect prior restraint comes in the form of a licensing scheme, under which expression is banned for want government permission as in *Freedman v. Maryland*, the scheme must include prompt judicial review at the petition and burden of the regulator.[118]

Yet, the courts have been unwilling to classify as constitutionally suspect all instances of apparent prior restraint. The government in its presentation to the Second Circuit pointed to a number of instances where withstanding an apparent prior restraint regulators were held to a less demanding standard—citing cases involving pre-trial discovery gag orders, grand jury secrecy, the confidentiality surrounding inquiry into judicial misconduct, and the secrecy agreements signed by national security employees.[119]

In fact when the Supreme Court assessed the First Amendment validity of a pre-trial discovery gag order, it concluded that the relevant questions were two: first, "whether the practice in question furthers an important or substantial governmental interest unrelated to the suppression of expression;" and second, "whether the limitation of First Amendment freedoms is no greater than is necessary or essential to the protection of the particular governmental interest involved."[120]

---

[114] *John Doe, Inc. v. Mukasey*, 549 F.3d at 883-84.

[115] *Doe v. Ashcroft*, 334 F.Supp.2d 471, 511 (S.D.N.Y. 2004); *Doe v. Gonzales*, 386 F.Supp.2d 66, 75 (D.Conn. 2005)("Section 2709(c) is subject to strict scrutiny not only because it is a prior restraint, but also because it is a content-based restriction").

[116] *Playboy Entertainment* 529 U.S. 803, 813 (2000).

[117] *Reno v. ACLU*, 521 U.S. 844, 874 (1997).

[118] *FW/PHS, Inc. v. Dallas*, 493 U.S. 215, (1990)("In *Freedman*, we determined that the following three procedural safeguards were necessary to ensure expeditious decisionmaking by the motion picture censorship board: (1) any restraint prior to judicial review can be imposed only for a specified brief period during which the status quo must be maintained; (2) expeditious judicial review of that decision must be available; and (3) the censor must bear the burden of proof once in court"), citing *Freedman v. Maryland*, 380 U.S. 51, 58-60 (1965).

[119] *John Doe, Inc. v. Mukasey*, 549 F.3d 861, 876-77 (2d Cir. 2008) noting the government contentions based on *Seattle Times Co. v. Rhinehard*, 467 U.S. 20 (1984)(pre-trial discovery); *Douglas Oil Co. v. Petrol Stops Northwest*, 441 U.S. 211 (1979)(grand jury); *Kamasinski v. Judicial Review Council*, 44 F.3d 106 (2d Cir. 1994)(judicial misconduct); *United States v. Snepp*, 897 F.2d 138 (4th Cir. 1990)(CIA employees); *United States v. Marchetti*, 466 F.2d 1309 (4th Cir. 1972)(same).

[120] *Seattle Times Co. v. Rhinehard*, 467 U.S. at 32.

The members of the Second Circuit panel could not agree on whether section 2709(c), as amended, constituted a prior restraint subject to strict scrutiny analysis, or should be judged by a somewhat less demanding standard. The lack of consensus proved of little consequence, because the government conceded that strict scrutiny analysis was appropriate,[121] and because the panel agreed the result would be the same under the factor common to both standards—whether the restriction on expression crafted to protect the government's interest was narrowly tailored for that purpose.[122]

The government's interest in national security is indisputably compelling.[123] Unwilling to read section 2709(c) procedure as a licensing scheme, the Second Circuit panel nevertheless concluded that "in the absence of Government-initiated judicial review, subsection 3511(b) is not narrowly tailored to conform to First Amendment protected standards."[124] Moreover, the judicial review must be real. It must "place on the Government the burden to show a good reason to believe that disclosure may result in an enumerated harm, *i.e.* a harm related to an authorized investigation to protect against international terrorism or clandestine intelligence activities."[125] Such judicial review may occur ex parte and in camera, but it may not be bound by the executive's conclusive certification of harm feature of section 3511. In the eyes of the court, there is no meaningful judicial review "of the decision of the Executive Branch to prohibit speech if the position of the Executive Branch that speech would be harmful is 'conclusive' on the reviewing court, absent only a demonstration of bad faith."[126] "To accept deference to that extraordinary degree would be to reduce strict scrutiny to no scrutiny, save only in the rarest of situations where bad faith could be shown," it concluded.[127]

Yet the court envisioned a procedure under which NSL secrecy provision might survive:

> We deem it beyond the authority of a court to "interpret" or "revise" the NSL statutes to create the constitutionally required obligation of the Government to initiate judicial review of a nondisclosure requirement. However, the Government might be able to assume such an obligation without additional legislation....
>
> If the Government uses the suggested reciprocal notice procedure as a means of initiating judicial review, there appears to be no impediment to the Government's including notice of a recipient's opportunity to contest the nondisclosure requirement in an NSL. If such notice is given, time limits on the nondisclosure requirement pending judicial review, as reflected in *Freedman*, would have to be applied to make the review procedure constitutional. We would deem it to be within our judicial authority to conform subsection 2709(c) to First Amendment requirements, by limiting the duration of the nondisclosure requirement, absent a ruling favorable to the Government upon judicial review, to the 10-day period in which the NSL recipient decides whether to contest the nondisclosure requirement, the 30-day period in which the Government considers whether to seek judicial review, and a further period of 60 days in which a court must adjudicate the merits, unless special circumstances warrant additional time. If the NSL recipient declines timely to precipitate Government-initiated

---

[121] *John Doe, Inc. v. Mukasey*, 549 F.3d at 878.

[122] *Id.*

[123] *John Doe, Inc. v. Mukasey*, 549 F.3d at 878, citing *Haig v. Agee*, 453 U.S. 280, 307 (1981).

[124] *John Doe, Inc. v. Mukasey*, 549 F.3d at 880-81.

[125] *Id.* at 881.

[126] *Id.* at 882.

[127] *Id.*

judicial review, the nondisclosure requirement would continue, subject to the recipient's existing opportunities for annual challenges to the nondisclosure requirement provided by subsection 3511(b). If such an annual challenge is made, the standards and burden of proof that we have specified for an initial challenge would apply, although the Government would not be obliged to initiate judicial review.[128]

Given the possibility of constitutional application, the court saw no reason to invalidate sections 2709(c) and 3511(b) in toto. The exclusive presumptions of section 3511 cannot survive, the court declared, but the First Amendment finds no offense in the remainder of the two sections except "to the extent that they fail to provide for Government-initiated judicial review. The Government can respond to this partial invalidation ruling by using the suggested reciprocal notice procedure."[129]

On remand under the procedure suggested by the Court of Appeals, the government submitted the declaration of the senior FBI official concerning the continued need for secrecy concerning the NSL. Following an ex parte, in camera hearing, the district court concluded the government had met its burden, but granted the plaintiff's motion for an unclassified, redacted summary of the FBI declaration.[130]

The possibility of a conflicting view has arisen in the Ninth Circuit. A federal district court there agreed with the Second Circuit that the NSL confidentiality and judicial review provisions were constitutionally suspect.[131] Yet it could not agree with the Second Circuit that NSL authority might be used if the confidentiality and judicial review provisions were implemented to satisfy constitutional demands. The statutory language was too clear and the congressional intent too apparent for the court to feel it could move in the opposite direction. It declared:

> The statutory provisions at issue—as written, adopted and amended by Congress in the face of a constitutional challenge—are not susceptible to narrowing conforming constructions to save their constitutionality ... [I]n amending and reenacting the statute as it did, Congress was concerned with giving the government the broadest powers possible to issue NSL nondisclosure orders and to preclude searching judicial review of the same ... [T]he sorts of multiple inferences required to save the provisions at issue are not only contrary to evidence of Congressional intent, but also contrary to the statutory language and structure of the statutory provisions actually enacted by Congress.[132]

The district court also concluded that, if the confidentiality and judicial review provisions could not survive, neither could the remainder of the NSL authority.[133] The court, therefore, barred the

---

[128] *Id.* at 883-84.

[129] *Id.* at 884.

[130] *Doe v. Holder*, 665 F.Supp.2d 426, 432-34 (S.D.N.Y. 2009); see also *Doe v. Holder*, 703 F.Supp.2d 313 (S.D.N.Y. 2010).

[131] *In re National Security Letter*, 930 F.Supp.2d 1064, 1081 (N.D.Cal. 2013)("[T]he Court concludes that the nondisclosure provision of 18 U.S.C. §2709(c) violates the First Amendment and 18 U.S.C. §3511(b)(2) and (b)(3) violate the Frist Amendment and separation of powers principles").

[132] *Id.* at 1080.

[133] *Id.* at 1081(internal citations omitted) ("The Court also finds that the unconstitutional nondisclosure provisions are not severable. There is ample evidence, in the manner in which the statutes were adopted and subsequently amended after their constitutionality was first rejected in *Doe v. Ashcroft* and *Doe v. Gonzales*, that Congress fully understood the issues at hand and the importance of the nondisclosure provisions. Moreover, it is hard to imagine how the substantive NSL provisions—which are important for national security purposes—could function if no recipient were required to abide by the nondisclosure provisions which have been issued in approximately 97% of the NSLs issued").

government from using Section 2709's NSL authority and from enforcing the related NSL confidentiality provisions. It stayed the order pending appeal.

Appendixes

(Language added by P.L. 109-177 (H.R. 3199): in italics)
(Language added by P.L. 109-178 (S. 2271): in bold)
(Language repealed by either: struck out)

12 U.S.C. 3414 (text)

(a)(1) Nothing in this chapter (except sections 3415, 3417, 3418, and 3421 of this title) shall apply to the production and disclosure of financial records pursuant to requests from:

(A) a Government authority authorized to conduct foreign counter- or foreign positive-intelligence activities for purposes of conducting such activities;

(B) the Secret Service for the purpose of conducting its protective functions (18 U.S.C. 3056; 3 U.S.C. 202, Public Law 90-331, as amended); or

(C) a Government authority authorized to conduct investigations of, or intelligence or counterintelligence analyses related to, international terrorism for the purpose of conducting such investigations or analyses.

(2) In the instances specified in paragraph (1), the Government authority shall submit to the financial institution the certificate required in section 3403(b) of this title signed by a supervisory official of a rank designated by the head of the Government authority.

(3) ~~No financial institution, or officer, employee, or agent of such institution, shall disclose to any person that a Government authority described in paragraph (1) has sought or obtained access to a customer's financial records.~~

(3)(A) If the Government authority described in paragraph (1) or the Secret Service, as the case may be, certifies that otherwise there may result a danger to the national security of the United States, interference with a criminal, counterterrorism, or counterintelligence investigation, interference with diplomatic relations, or danger to the life or physical safety of any person, no financial institution, or officer, employee, or agent of such institution, shall disclose to any person (other than those to whom such disclosure is necessary to comply with the request or an attorney to obtain legal advice or legal assistance with respect to the request) that the Government authority or the Secret Service has sought or obtained access to a customer's financial records.

(B) The request shall notify the person or entity to whom the request is directed of the nondisclosure requirement under subparagraph (A).

(C) Any recipient disclosing to those persons necessary to comply with the request or to an attorney to obtain legal advice or legal assistance with respect to the request shall inform such persons of any applicable nondisclosure requirement. Any person who receives a disclosure under this subsection shall be subject to the same prohibitions on disclosure under subparagraph (A).

(D) At the request of the authorized Government agency or the Secret Service, any person making or intending to make a disclosure under this section shall identify to the requesting official of the authorized Government agency or the Secret Service the person to whom such disclosure will be made or to whom such disclosure was made prior to the request, [~~but in no circumstance shall a person be required to inform such requesting official that the person intends to consult an attorney to obtain legal advice or legal assistance~~] **except that nothing in this section shall require a person to inform the requesting official of the authorized Government authority or the Secret Service of the identity of an attorney to whom**

disclosure was made or will be made to obtain legal advice or legal assistance with respect to the request for financial records under this subsection.

(4) The Government authority specified in paragraph (1) shall compile an annual tabulation of the occasions in which this section was used.

(5)(A) Financial institutions, and officers, employees, and agents thereof, shall comply with a request for a customer's or entity's financial records made pursuant to this subsection by the Federal Bureau of Investigation when the Director of the Federal Bureau of Investigation (or the Director's designee in a position not lower than Deputy Assistant Director at Bureau headquarters or a Special Agent in Charge in a Bureau field office designated by the Director) certifies in writing to the financial institution that such records are sought for foreign counter intelligence purposes to protect against international terrorism or clandestine intelligence activities, provided that such an investigation of a United States person is not conducted solely upon the basis of activities protected by the first amendment to the Constitution of the United States.

(B) The Federal Bureau of Investigation may disseminate information obtained pursuant to this paragraph only as provided in guidelines approved by the Attorney General for foreign intelligence collection and foreign counterintelligence investigations conducted by the Federal Bureau of Investigation, and, with respect to dissemination to an agency of the United States, only if such information is clearly relevant to the authorized responsibilities of such agency.

(C) On the dates provided in section 415b of Title 50, the Attorney General shall fully inform the congressional intelligence committees (as defined in section 401a of Title 50) concerning all requests made pursuant to this paragraph.

(D) No prohibition of certain disclosure.—

~~No financial institution, or officer, employee, or agent of such institution, shall disclose to any person that the Federal Bureau of Investigation has sought or obtained access to a customer's or entity's financial records under this paragraph.~~

(i) If the Director of the Federal Bureau of Investigation, or his designee in a position not lower than Deputy Assistant Director at Bureau headquarters or a Special Agent in Charge in a Bureau field office designated by the Director, certifies that otherwise there may result a danger to the national security of the United States, interference with a criminal, counterterrorism, or counterintelligence investigation, interference with diplomatic relations, or danger to the life or physical safety of any person, no financial institution, or officer, employee, or agent of such institution, shall disclose to any person (other than those to whom such disclosure is necessary to comply with the request or an attorney to obtain legal advice or legal assistance with respect to the request) that the Federal Bureau of Investigation has sought or obtained access to a customer's or entity's financial records under subparagraph (A).

(ii) The request shall notify the person or entity to whom the request is directed of the nondisclosure requirement under clause (i).

(iii) Any recipient disclosing to those persons necessary to comply with the request or to an attorney to obtain legal advice or legal assistance with respect to the request shall inform such persons of any applicable nondisclosure requirement. Any person who receives a disclosure under this subsection shall be subject to the same prohibitions on disclosure under clause (i).

(iv) At the request of the Director of the Federal Bureau of Investigation or the designee of the Director, any person making or intending to make a disclosure under this section shall identify to the Director or such designee the person to whom such disclosure will be made or to whom such disclosure was made prior to the request, [~~but in no circumstance shall a person be required to inform the Director or such designee that the person intends to consult an attorney to obtain legal advice or legal assistance~~] **except that nothing in**

this section shall require a person to inform the Director or such designee of the identity of an attorney to whom disclosure was made or will be made to obtain legal advice or legal assistance with respect to the request for financial records under subparagraph (A).

(b)(1) Nothing in this chapter shall prohibit a Government authority from obtaining financial records from a financial institution if the Government authority determines that delay in obtaining access to such records would create imminent danger of—

    (A) physical injury to any person;

    (B) serious property damage; or

    (C) flight to avoid prosecution.

(2) In the instances specified in paragraph (1), the Government shall submit to the financial institution the certificate required in section 3403(b) of this title signed by a supervisory official of a rank designated by the head of the Government authority.

(3) Within five days of obtaining access to financial records under this subsection, the Government authority shall file with the appropriate court a signed, sworn statement of a supervisory official of a rank designated by the head of the Government authority setting forth the grounds for the emergency access. The Government authority shall thereafter comply with the notice provisions of section 3409(c) of this title.

(4) The Government authority specified in paragraph (1) shall compile an annual tabulation of the occasions in which this section was used.

[there is no subsection (c)]

(d) For purposes of this section, and sections 1115 and 1117 [12 U.S.C. 3415, 3417 relating to cost reimbursement and civil penalties respectively] insofar as they relate to the operation of this section, the term "financial institution" has the same meaning as in subsections (a)(2) and (c)(1) of section 5312 of title 31, United States Code, except that, for purposes of this section, such term shall include only such a financial institution any part of which is located inside any State or territory of the United States, the District of Columbia, Puerto Rico, Guam, American Samoa, the Commonwealth of the Northern Mariana Islands, or the United States Virgin Islands. [Subsection (d) was added by subsection 374(a) of the Intelligence Authorization Act for Fiscal Year 2004, P.L. 108-177, 117 Stat. 2628 (2003).]

18 U.S.C. 2709 (text)

(a) Duty to provide.—A wire or electronic communication service provider shall comply with a request for subscriber information and toll billing records information, or electronic communication transactional records in its custody or possession made by the Director of the Federal Bureau of Investigation under subsection (b) of this section.

(b) Required certification.—The Director of the Federal Bureau of Investigation, or his designee in a position not lower than Deputy Assistant Director at Bureau headquarters or a Special Agent in Charge in a Bureau field office designated by the Director, may—

(1) request the name, address, length of service, and local and long distance toll billing records of a person or entity if the Director (or his designee) certifies in writing to the wire or electronic communication service provider to which the request is made that the name, address, length of service, and toll billing records sought are relevant to an authorized investigation to protect against international terrorism or clandestine intelligence activities, provided that such an investigation of a United States person is not conducted solely on the basis of activities protected by the first amendment to the Constitution of the United States; and

(2) request the name, address, and length of service of a person or entity if the Director (or his designee) certifies in writing to the wire or electronic communication service provider to which the request is made that the information sought is relevant to an authorized investigation to protect against international terrorism or clandestine intelligence activities, provided that such an investigation of a United States person is not conducted solely upon the basis of activities protected by the first amendment to the Constitution of the United States.

(c) Prohibition of certain disclosure.— ~~No wire or electronic communication service provider, or officer, employee, or agent thereof, shall disclose to any person that the Federal Bureau of Investigation has sought or obtained access to information or records under this section.~~

(1) If the Director of the Federal Bureau of Investigation, or his designee in a position not lower than Deputy Assistant Director at Bureau headquarters or a Special Agent in Charge in a Bureau field office designated by the Director, certifies that otherwise there may result a danger to the national security of the United States, interference with a criminal, counterterrorism, or counterintelligence investigation, interference with diplomatic relations, or danger to the life or physical safety of any person, no wire or electronic communications service provider, or officer, employee, or agent thereof, shall disclose to any person (other than those to whom such disclosure is necessary to comply with the request or an attorney to obtain legal advice or legal assistance with respect to the request) that the Federal Bureau of Investigation has sought or obtained access to information or records under this section.

(2) The request shall notify the person or entity to whom the request is directed of the nondisclosure requirement under paragraph (1).

(3) Any recipient disclosing to those persons necessary to comply with the request or to an attorney to obtain legal advice or legal assistance with respect to the request shall inform such person of any applicable nondisclosure requirement. Any person who receives a disclosure under this subsection shall be subject to the same prohibitions on disclosure under paragraph (1).

(4) At the request of the Director of the Federal Bureau of Investigation or the designee of the Director, any person making or intending to make a disclosure under this section shall identify to the Director or such designee the person to whom such disclosure will be made or to whom such disclosure was made prior to the request, [~~but in no circumstance shall a person be required to inform the Director or such designee that the person intends to consult an attorney to obtain legal advice or legal assistance~~] **except that nothing in this section shall require a person to inform the Director or such designee of the identity of an attorney to whom disclosure was made or will be made to obtain legal advice or legal assistance with respect to the request under subsection (a).**

(d) Dissemination by bureau.—The Federal Bureau of Investigation may disseminate information and records obtained under this section only as provided in guidelines approved by the Attorney General for foreign intelligence collection and foreign counterintelligence investigations conducted by the Federal Bureau of Investigation, and, with respect to dissemination to an agency of the United States, only if such information is clearly relevant to the authorized responsibilities of such agency.

(e) Requirement that certain congressional bodies be informed.—On a semiannual basis the Director of the Federal Bureau of Investigation shall fully inform the Permanent Select Committee on Intelligence of the House of Representatives and the Select Committee on Intelligence of the Senate, and the Committee on the Judiciary of the House of Representatives and the Committee on the Judiciary of the Senate, concerning all requests made under subsection (b) of this section.

(f) Libraries- A library (as that term is defined in section 213(1) of the Library Services and Technology Act (20 U.S.C. 9122(1)), the services of which include access to the Internet,

books, journals, magazines, newspapers, or other similar forms of communication in print or digitally by patrons for their use, review, examination, or circulation, is not a wire or electronic communication service provider for purposes of this section, unless the library is providing the services defined in section 2510(15) (`electronic communication service') of this title.

15 U.S.C. 1681u (text)

(a) Identity of financial institutions

Notwithstanding section 1681b of this title or any other provision of this subchapter, a consumer reporting agency shall furnish to the Federal Bureau of Investigation the names and addresses of all financial institutions (as that term is defined in section 3401 of Title 12) at which a consumer maintains or has maintained an account, to the extent that information is in the files of the agency, when presented with a written request for that information, signed by the Director of the Federal Bureau of Investigation, or the Director's designee in a position not lower than Deputy Assistant Director at Bureau headquarters or a Special Agent in Charge of a Bureau field office designated by the Director, which certifies compliance with this section. The Director or the Director's designee may make such a certification only if the Director or the Director's designee has determined in writing, that such information is sought for the conduct of an authorized investigation to protect against international terrorism or clandestine intelligence activities, provided that such an investigation of a United States person is not conducted solely upon the basis of activities protected by the first amendment to the Constitution of the United States.

(b) Identifying information

Notwithstanding the provisions of section 1681b of this title or any other provision of this subchapter, a consumer reporting agency shall furnish identifying information respecting a consumer, limited to name, address, former addresses, places of employment, or former places of employment, to the Federal Bureau of Investigation when presented with a written request, signed by the Director or the Director's designee in a position not lower than Deputy Assistant Director at Bureau headquarters or a Special Agent in Charge of a Bureau field office designated by the Director, which certifies compliance with this subsection. The Director or the Director's designee may make such a certification only if the Director or the Director's designee has determined in writing that such information is sought for the conduct of an authorized investigation to protect against international terrorism or clandestine intelligence activities, provided that such an investigation of a United States person is not conducted solely upon the basis of activities protected by the first amendment to the Constitution of the United States.

(c) Court order for disclosure of consumer reports

Notwithstanding section 1681b of this title or any other provision of this subchapter, if requested in writing by the Director of the Federal Bureau of Investigation, or a designee of the Director in a position not lower than Deputy Assistant Director at Bureau headquarters or a Special Agent in Charge in a Bureau field office designated by the Director, a court may issue an order ex parte directing a consumer reporting agency to furnish a consumer report to the Federal Bureau of Investigation, upon a showing in camera that the consumer report is sought for the conduct of an authorized investigation to protect against international terrorism or clandestine intelligence activities, provided that such an investigation of a United States person is not conducted solely upon the basis of activities protected by the first amendment to the Constitution of the United States.

The terms of an order issued under this subsection shall not disclose that the order is issued for purposes of a counterintelligence investigation.

(d) Confidentiality

~~No consumer reporting agency or officer, employee, or agent of a consumer reporting agency shall disclose to any person, other than those officers, employees, or agents of a consumer reporting agency necessary to fulfill the requirement to disclose information to the Federal Bureau of Investigation under this section, that the Federal Bureau of Investigation has sought or obtained the identity of financial institutions or a consumer report respecting any consumer under subsection (a), (b), or (c) of this section, and no consumer reporting agency or officer, employee, or agent of a consumer reporting agency shall include in any consumer report any information that would indicate that the Federal Bureau of Investigation has sought or obtained such information or a consumer report.~~

(1) If the Director of the Federal Bureau of Investigation, or his designee in a position not lower than Deputy Assistant Director at Bureau headquarters or a Special Agent in Charge in a Bureau field office designated by the Director, certifies that otherwise there may result a danger to the national security of the United States, interference with a criminal, counterterrorism, or counterintelligence investigation, interference with diplomatic relations, or danger to the life or physical safety of any person, no consumer reporting agency or officer, employee, or agent of a consumer reporting agency shall disclose to any person (other than those to whom such disclosure is necessary to comply with the request or an attorney to obtain legal advice or legal assistance with respect to the request) that the Federal Bureau of Investigation has sought or obtained the identity of financial institutions or a consumer report respecting any consumer under subsection (a), (b), or (c), and no consumer reporting agency or officer, employee, or agent of a consumer reporting agency shall include in any consumer report any information that would indicate that the Federal Bureau of Investigation has sought or obtained such information on a consumer report.

(2) The request shall notify the person or entity to whom the request is directed of the nondisclosure requirement under paragraph (1).

(3) Any recipient disclosing to those persons necessary to comply with the request or to an attorney to obtain legal advice or legal assistance with respect to the request shall inform such persons of any applicable nondisclosure requirement. Any person who receives a disclosure under this subsection shall be subject to the same prohibitions on disclosure under paragraph (1).

(4) At the request of the Director of the Federal Bureau of Investigation or the designee of the Director, any person making or intending to make a disclosure under this section shall identify to the Director or such designee the person to whom such disclosure will be made or to whom such disclosure was made prior to the request,[~~*but in no circumstance shall a person be required to inform the Director or such designee that the person intends to consult an attorney to obtain legal advice or legal assistance*~~*]* **except that nothing in this section shall require a person to inform the Director or such designee of the identity of an attorney to whom disclosure was made or will be made to obtain legal advice or legal assistance with respect to the request for the identity of financial institutions or a consumer report respecting any consumer under this section.**

(e) Payment of fees

The Federal Bureau of Investigation shall, subject to the availability of appropriations, pay to the consumer reporting agency assembling or providing report or information in accordance with procedures established under this section a fee for reimbursement for such costs as are reasonably necessary and which have been directly incurred in searching, reproducing, or transporting books, papers, records, or other data required or requested to be produced under this section.

(f) Limit on dissemination

The Federal Bureau of Investigation may not disseminate information obtained pursuant to this section outside of the Federal Bureau of Investigation, except to other Federal agencies as may be necessary for the approval or conduct of a foreign counterintelligence investigation, or, where the information concerns a person subject to the Uniform Code of Military Justice, to appropriate investigative authorities within the military department concerned as may be necessary for the conduct of a joint foreign counterintelligence investigation.

(g) Rules of construction
 Nothing in this section shall be construed to prohibit information from being furnished by the Federal Bureau of Investigation pursuant to a subpoena or court order, in connection with a judicial or administrative proceeding to enforce the provisions of this subchapter. Nothing in this section shall be construed to authorize or permit the withholding of information from the Congress.

(h) Reports to Congress
 (1) On a semiannual basis, the Attorney General shall fully inform the Permanent Select Committee on Intelligence and the Committee on Banking, Finance and Urban Affairs of the House of Representatives, and the Select Committee on Intelligence and the Committee on Banking, Housing, and Urban Affairs of the Senate concerning all requests made pursuant to subsections (a), (b), and (c) of this section.
 (2) In the case of the semiannual reports required to be submitted under paragraph (1) to the Permanent Select Committee on Intelligence of the House of Representatives and the Select Committee on Intelligence of the Senate, the submittal dates for such reports shall be as provided in section 415b of Title 50.

(i) Damages
 Any agency or department of the United States obtaining or disclosing any consumer reports, records, or information contained therein in violation of this section is liable to the consumer to whom such consumer reports, records, or information relate in an amount equal to the sum of—
 (1) $100, without regard to the volume of consumer reports, records, or information involved;
 (2) any actual damages sustained by the consumer as a result of the disclosure;
 (3) if the violation is found to have been willful or intentional, such punitive damages as a court may allow; and
 (4) in the case of any successful action to enforce liability under this subsection, the costs of the action, together with reasonable attorney fees, as determined by the court.

(j) Disciplinary actions for violations
 If a court determines that any agency or department of the United States has violated any provision of this section and the court finds that the circumstances surrounding the violation raise questions of whether or not an officer or employee of the agency or department acted willfully or intentionally with respect to the violation, the agency or department shall promptly initiate a proceeding to determine whether or not disciplinary action is warranted against the officer or employee who was responsible for the violation.
(k) Good-faith exception
 Notwithstanding any other provision of this subchapter, any consumer reporting agency or agent or employee thereof making disclosure of consumer reports or identifying information pursuant to this subsection in good-faith reliance upon a certification of the Federal Bureau of Investigation pursuant to provisions of this section shall not be liable to any person for such disclosure under this subchapter, the constitution of any State, or any law or regulation of any State or any political subdivision of any State.

(l) Limitation of remedies

Notwithstanding any other provision of this subchapter, the remedies and sanctions set forth in this section shall be the only judicial remedies and sanctions for violation of this section.

(m) Injunctive relief

In addition to any other remedy contained in this section, injunctive relief shall be available to require compliance with the procedures of this section. In the event of any successful action under this subsection, costs together with reasonable attorney fees, as determined by the court, may be recovered.

15 U.S.C. 1681v (text)

(a) Disclosure

Notwithstanding section 1681b of this title or any other provision of this subchapter, a consumer reporting agency shall furnish a consumer report of a consumer and all other information in a consumer's file to a government agency authorized to conduct investigations of, or intelligence or counterintelligence activities or analysis related to, international terrorism when presented with a written certification by such government agency that such information is necessary for the agency's conduct or such investigation, activity or analysis.

(b) Form of certification

The certification described in subsection (a) shall be signed by a supervisory official designated by the head of a Federal agency or an officer of a Federal agency whose appointment to office is required to be made by the President, by and with the advice and consent of the Senate.

(c) Confidentiality

~~No consumer reporting agency, or officer, employee, or agent of such consumer reporting agency, shall disclose to any person, or specify in any consumer report, that a government agency has sought or obtained access to information under subsection (a).~~

(1) If the head of a government agency authorized to conduct investigations of intelligence or counterintelligence activities or analysis related to international terrorism, or his designee, certifies that otherwise there may result a danger to the national security of the United States, interference with a criminal, counterterrorism, or counterintelligence investigation, interference with diplomatic relations, or danger to the life or physical safety of any person, no consumer reporting agency or officer, employee, or agent of such consumer reporting agency, shall disclose to any person (other than those to whom such disclosure is necessary to comply with the request or an attorney to obtain legal advice or legal assistance with respect to the request), or specify in any consumer report, that a government agency has sought or obtained access to information under subsection (a).

(2) The request shall notify the person or entity to whom the request is directed of the nondisclosure requirement under paragraph (1).

(3) Any recipient disclosing to those persons necessary to comply with the request or to any attorney to obtain legal advice or legal assistance with respect to the request shall inform such persons of any applicable nondisclosure requirement. Any person who receives a disclosure under this subsection shall be subject to the same prohibitions on disclosure under paragraph (1).

(4) At the request of the authorized Government agency, any person making or intending to make a disclosure under this section shall identify to the requesting official of the authorized Government agency the person to whom such disclosure will be made or to whom such disclosure was made prior to the request, [~~but in no circumstance shall a person be required to inform such~~

~~*requesting official that the person intends to consult an attorney to obtain legal advice or legal assistance]*~~ **except that nothing in this section shall require a person to inform the requesting official of the identity of an attorney to whom disclosure was made or will be made to obtain legal advice or legal assistance with respect to the request for information under subsection (a).**

(d) Rule of construction

Nothing in section 1681u of this title shall be construed to limit the authority of the Director of the Federal Bureau of Investigation under this section.

(e) Safe harbor

Notwithstanding any other provision of this subchapter, any consumer reporting agency or agent or employee thereof making disclosure of consumer reports or other information pursuant to this section in good-faith reliance upon a certification of a governmental agency pursuant to the provisions of this section shall not be liable to any person for such disclosure under this subchapter, the constitution of any State, or any law or regulation of any State or any political subdivision of any State.

(f) Reports to Congress- (1) On a semi-annual basis, the Attorney General shall fully inform the Committee on the Judiciary, the Committee on Financial Services, and the Permanent Select Committee on Intelligence of the House of Representatives and the Committee on the Judiciary, the Committee on Banking, Housing, and Urban Affairs, and the Select Committee on Intelligence of the Senate concerning all requests made pursuant to subsection (a).

(2) In the case of the semiannual reports required to be submitted under paragraph (1) to the Permanent Select Committee on Intelligence of the House of Representatives and the Select Committee on Intelligence of the Senate, the submittal dates for such reports shall be as provided in section 507 of the National Security Act of 1947 (50 U.S.C. 415b).

Section 802 of the National Security Act (50 U.S.C. 3162) (text)

(a) Generally

(1) Any authorized investigative agency may request from any financial agency, financial institution, or holding company, or from any consumer reporting agency, such financial records, other financial information, and consumer reports as may be necessary in order to conduct any authorized law enforcement investigation, counterintelligence inquiry, or security determination. Any authorized investigative agency may also request records maintained by any commercial entity within the United States pertaining to travel by an employee in the executive branch of Government outside the United States.

(2) Requests may be made under this section where—

(A) the records sought pertain to a person who is or was an employee in the executive branch of Government required by the President in an Executive order or regulation, as a condition of access to classified information, to provide consent, during a background investigation and for such time as access to the information is maintained, and for a period of not more than three years thereafter, permitting access to financial records, other financial information, consumer reports, and travel records; and

(B)(i) there are reasonable grounds to believe, based on credible information, that the person is, or may be, disclosing classified information in an unauthorized manner to a foreign power or agent of a foreign power;

(ii) information the employing agency deems credible indicates the person has incurred excessive indebtedness or has acquired a level of affluence which cannot be explained by other information known to the agency; or

(iii) circumstances indicate the person had the capability and opportunity to disclose classified information which is known to have been lost or compromised to a foreign power or an agent of a foreign power.

(3) Each such request—

(A) shall be accompanied by a written certification signed by the department or agency head or deputy department or agency head concerned, or by a senior official designated for this purpose by the department or agency head concerned (whose rank shall be no lower than Assistant Secretary or Assistant Director), and shall certify that—

(i) the person concerned is or was an employee within the meaning of paragraph (2)(A);

(ii) the request is being made pursuant to an authorized inquiry or investigation and is authorized under this section; and

(iii) the records or information to be reviewed are records or information which the employee has previously agreed to make available to the authorized investigative agency for review;

(B) shall contain a copy of the agreement referred to in subparagraph (A)(iii);

(C) shall identify specifically or by category the records or information to be reviewed; and

(D) shall inform the recipient of the request of the prohibition described in subsection (b) of this section.

(b) Disclosure of requests

~~Notwithstanding any other provision of law, no governmental or private entity, or officer, employee, or agent of such entity, may disclose to any person, other than those officers, employees, or agents of such entity necessary to satisfy a request made under this section, that such entity has received or satisfied a request made by an authorized investigative agency under this section.~~

(1) If an authorized investigative agency described in subsection (a) certifies that otherwise there may result a danger to the national security of the United States, interference with a criminal, counterterrorism, or counterintelligence investigation, interference with diplomatic relations, or danger to the life or physical safety of any person, no governmental or private entity, or officer, employee, or agent of such entity, may disclose to any person (other than those to whom such disclosure is necessary to comply with the request or an attorney to obtain legal advice or legal assistance with respect to the request) that such entity has received or satisfied a request made by an authorized investigative agency under this section.

(2) The request shall notify the person or entity to whom the request is directed of the nondisclosure requirement under paragraph (1).

(3) Any recipient disclosing to those persons necessary to comply with the request or to an attorney to obtain legal advice or legal assistance with respect to the request shall inform such persons of any applicable nondisclosure requirement. Any person who receives a disclosure under this subsection shall be subject to the same prohibitions on disclosure under paragraph (1).

(4) At the request of the authorized investigative agency, any person making or intending to make a disclosure under this section shall identify to the requesting official of the authorized investigative agency the person to whom such disclosure will be made or to whom such disclosure was made prior to the request, [~~but in no circumstance shall a person be required to inform such official that the person intends to consult an attorney to obtain legal advice or legal assistance~~] **except that nothing in this section shall require a person to inform the requesting official of the identity of an attorney to whom disclosure was made or will be made to obtain legal advice or legal assistance with respect to the request under subsection (a).**

(c) Records or information; inspection or copying

(1) Notwithstanding any other provision of law (other than section 6103 of Title 26), an entity receiving a request for records or information under subsection (a) of this section shall, if the request satisfies the requirements of this section, make available such records or information within 30 days for inspection or copying, as may be appropriate, by the agency requesting such records or information.

(2) Any entity (including any officer, employee, or agent thereof) that discloses records or information for inspection or copying pursuant to this section in good faith reliance upon the certifications made by an agency pursuant to this section shall not be liable for any such disclosure to any person under this subchapter, the constitution of any State, or any law or regulation of any State or any political subdivision of any State.

(d) Reimbursement of costs

Any agency requesting records or information under this section may, subject to the availability of appropriations, reimburse a private entity for any cost reasonably incurred by such entity in responding to such request, including the cost of identifying, reproducing, or transporting records or other data.

(e) Dissemination of records or information received

An agency receiving records or information pursuant to a request under this section may disseminate the records or information obtained pursuant to such request outside the agency only—

(1) to the agency employing the employee who is the subject of the records or information;

(2) to the Department of Justice for law enforcement or counterintelligence purposes; or

(3) with respect to dissemination to an agency of the United States, if such information is clearly relevant to the authorized responsibilities of such agency.

(f) Construction of section

Nothing in this section may be construed to affect the authority of an investigative agency to obtain information pursuant to the Right to Financial Privacy Act (12 U.S.C. 3401 et seq.) or the Fair Credit Reporting Act (15 U.S.C. 1681 et seq.).

18 U.S.C. 1510 (text)

* * *

(e) Whoever, having been notified of the applicable disclosure prohibitions or confidentiality requirements of section 2709(c)(1) of this title, section 626(d)(1) or 627(c)(1) of the Fair Credit Reporting Act (15 U.S.C. 1681u(d)(1) or 1681v(c)(1)), section 1114(a)(3)(A) or 1114(a)(5)(D)(i) of the Right to Financial Privacy Act (12 U.S.C. 3414(a)(3)(A) or 3414(a)(5)(D)(i)), or section 802(b)(1) of the National Security Act of 1947 (50 U.S.C. [3162](b)(1)), knowingly and with the intent to obstruct an investigation or judicial proceeding violates such prohibitions or requirements applicable by law to such person shall be imprisoned for not more than five years, fined under this title, or both.

P.L. 109-177, Section 118 (text)

Reports on National Security Letters.

(a) Existing Reports—Any report made to a committee of Congress regarding national security letters under section 2709(c)(1) of title 18, United States Code, sections 626(d) or 627(c) of the Fair Credit Reporting Act (15 U.S.C. 1681u(d) or 1681v(c)), section 1114(a)(3) or 1114(a)(5)(D) of the Right to Financial Privacy Act (12 U.S.C. 3414(a)(3) or 3414(a)(5)(D)), or section 802(b) of the National Security Act of 1947 (50 U.S.C. [3162](b)) shall also be made to the Committees on the Judiciary of the House of Representatives and the Senate.

* * *

(c) Report on Requests for National Security Letters-
(1) IN GENERAL- In April of each year, the Attorney General shall submit to Congress an aggregate report setting forth with respect to the preceding year the total number of requests made by the Department of Justice for information concerning different United States persons under—
   (A) section 2709 of title 18, United States Code (to access certain communication service provider records), excluding the number of requests for subscriber information;
   (B) section 1114 of the Right to Financial Privacy Act (12 U.S.C. 3414) (to obtain financial institution customer records);
   (C) section 802 of the National Security Act of 1947 (50 U.S.C. [3162]) (to obtain financial information, records, and consumer reports);
   (D) section 626 of the Fair Credit Reporting Act (15 U.S.C. 1681u) (to obtain certain financial information and consumer reports); and
   (E) section 627 of the Fair Credit Reporting Act (15 U.S.C. 1681v) (to obtain credit agency consumer records for counterterrorism investigations).
(2) UNCLASSIFIED FORM- The report under this section shall be submitted in unclassified form.

(d) National Security Letter Defined- In this section, the term 'national security letter' means a request for information under one of the following provisions of law:
(1) Section 2709(a) of title 18, United States Code (to access certain communication service provider records).
(2) Section 1114(a)(5)(A) of the Right to Financial Privacy Act (12 U.S.C. 3414(a)(5)(A)) (to obtain financial institution customer records).
(3) Section 802 of the National Security Act of 1947 (50 U.S.C.[3162]) (to obtain financial information, records, and consumer reports).
(4) Section 626 of the Fair Credit Reporting Act (15 U.S.C. 1681u) (to obtain certain financial information and consumer reports).
(5) Section 627 of the Fair Credit Reporting Act (15 U.S.C. 1681v) (to obtain credit agency consumer records for counterterrorism investigations).

P.L. 109-177, Section 119 (text)

Audit of Use of National Security Letters.

(a) Audit—The Inspector General of the Department of Justice shall perform an audit of the effectiveness and use, including any improper or illegal use, of national security letters issued by the Department of Justice.

(b) Requirements- The audit required under subsection (a) shall include—

(1) an examination of the use of national security letters by the Department of Justice during calendar years 2003 through 2006;

(2) a description of any noteworthy facts or circumstances relating to such use, including any improper or illegal use of such authority; and

(3) an examination of the effectiveness of national security letters as an investigative tool, including—

(A) the importance of the information acquired by the Department of Justice to the intelligence activities of the Department of Justice or to any other department or agency of the Federal Government;

(B) the manner in which such information is collected, retained, analyzed, and disseminated by the Department of Justice, including any direct access to such information (such as access to 'raw data') provided to any other department, agency, or instrumentality of Federal, State, local, or tribal governments or any private sector entity;

(C) whether, and how often, the Department of Justice utilized such information to produce an analytical intelligence product for distribution within the Department of Justice, to the intelligence community (as such term is defined in section 3(4) of the National Security Act of 1947 (50 U.S.C. 401a(4))), or to other Federal, State, local, or tribal government departments, agencies, or instrumentalities;

(D) whether, and how often, the Department of Justice provided such information to law enforcement authorities for use in criminal proceedings;

(E) with respect to national security letters issued following the date of the enactment of this Act, an examination of the number of occasions in which the Department of Justice, or an officer or employee of the Department of Justice, issued a national security letter without the certification necessary to require the recipient of such letter to comply with the nondisclosure and confidentiality requirements potentially applicable under law; and

(F) the types of electronic communications and transactional information obtained through requests for information under section 2709 of title 18, United States Code, including the types of dialing, routing, addressing, or signaling information obtained, and the procedures the Department of Justice uses if content information is obtained through the use of such authority.

(c) Submission Dates-

(1) PRIOR YEARS- Not later than one year after the date of the enactment of this Act, or upon completion of the audit under this section for calendar years 2003 and 2004, whichever is earlier, the Inspector General of the Department of Justice shall submit to the Committee on the Judiciary and the Permanent Select Committee on Intelligence of the House of Representatives and the Committee on the Judiciary and the Select Committee on Intelligence of the Senate a report containing the results of the audit conducted under this subsection for calendar years 2003 and 2004.

(2) CALENDAR YEARS 2005 AND 2006- Not later than December 31, 2007, or upon completion of the audit under this subsection for calendar years 2005 and 2006, whichever is earlier, the Inspector General of the Department of Justice shall submit to the Committee on the Judiciary and the Permanent Select Committee on Intelligence of the House of Representatives and the Committee on the Judiciary and the Select Committee on Intelligence of the Senate a report containing the results of the audit conducted under this subsection for calendar years 2005 and 2006.

(d) Prior Notice to Attorney General and Director of National Intelligence; Comments-

(1) NOTICE- Not less than 30 days before the submission of a report under subsections (c)(1) or (c)(2), the Inspector General of the Department of Justice shall provide such report to the Attorney General and the Director of National Intelligence.
(2) COMMENTS- The Attorney General or the Director of National Intelligence may provide comments to be included in the reports submitted under subsections (c)(1) or (c)(2) as the Attorney General or the Director of National Intelligence may consider necessary.

(e) Unclassified Form- The reports submitted under subsections (c)(1) or (c)(2) and any comments included under subsection (d)(2) shall be in unclassified form, but may include a classified annex.

(f) Minimization Procedures Feasibility- Not later than February 1, 2007, or upon completion of review of the report submitted under subsection (c)(1), whichever is earlier, the Attorney General and the Director of National Intelligence shall jointly submit to the Committee on the Judiciary and the Permanent Select Committee on Intelligence of the House of Representatives and the Committee on the Judiciary and the Select Committee on Intelligence of the Senate a report on the feasibility of applying minimization procedures in the context of national security letters to ensure the protection of the constitutional rights of United States persons.

(g) National Security Letter Defined- In this section, the term 'national security letter' means a request for information under one of the following provisions of law:
(1) Section 2709(a) of title 18, United States Code (to access certain communication service provider records).
(2) Section 1114(a)(5)(A) of the Right to Financial Privacy Act (12 U.S.C. 3414(a)(5)(A)) (to obtain financial institution customer records).
(3) Section 802 of the National Security Act of 1947 (50 U.S.C. 436) (to obtain financial information, records, and consumer reports).
(4) Section 626 of the Fair Credit Reporting Act (15 U.S.C. 1681u) (to obtain certain financial information and consumer reports).
(5) Section 627 of the Fair Credit Reporting Act (15 U.S.C. 1681v) (to obtain credit agency consumer records for counterterrorism investigations).

18 U.S.C. 3511 (text)

(a) The recipient of a request for records, a report, or other information under section 2709(b) of this title, section 626(a) or (b) or 627(a) of the Fair Credit Reporting Act, section 1114(a)(5)(A) of the Right to Financial Privacy Act, or section 802(a) of the National Security Act of 1947 may, in the United States district court for the district in which that person or entity does business or resides, petition for an order modifying or setting aside the request. The court may modify or set aside the request if compliance would be unreasonable, oppressive, or otherwise unlawful.

(b)(1) The recipient of a request for records, a report, or other information under section 2709(b) of this title, section 626(a) or (b) or 627(a) of the Fair Credit Reporting Act, section 1114(a)(5)(A) of the Right to Financial Privacy Act, or section 802(a) of the National Security Act of 1947, may petition any court described in subsection (a) for an order modifying or setting aside a nondisclosure requirement imposed in connection with such a request.
(2) If the petition is filed within one year of the request for records, a report, or other information under section 2709(b) of this title, section 626(a) or (b) or 627(a) of the Fair Credit Reporting Act, section 1114(a)(5)(A) of the Right to Financial Privacy Act, or section 802(a) of the National Security Act of 1947, the court may modify or set aside such a nondisclosure requirement if it finds that there is no reason to believe that disclosure may endanger the national security of the United States, interfere with a criminal, counterterrorism, or counterintelligence investigation,

interfere with diplomatic relations, or endanger the life or physical safety of any person. If, at the time of the petition, the Attorney General, Deputy Attorney General, an Assistant Attorney General, or the Director of the Federal Bureau of Investigation, or in the case of a request by a department, agency, or instrumentality of the Federal Government other than the Department of Justice, the head or deputy head of such department, agency, or instrumentality, certifies that disclosure may endanger the national security of the United States or interfere with diplomatic relations, such certification shall be treated as conclusive unless the court finds that the certification was made in bad faith.

(3) If the petition is filed one year or more after the request for records, a report, or other information under section 2709(b) of this title, section 626(a) or (b) or 627(a) of the Fair Credit Reporting Act, section 1114 (a)(5)(A) of the Right to Financial Privacy Act, or section 802(a) of the National Security Act of 1947, the Attorney General, Deputy Attorney General, an Assistant Attorney General, or the Director of the Federal Bureau of Investigation, or his designee in a position not lower than Deputy Assistant Director at Bureau headquarters or a Special Agent in Charge in a Bureau field office designated by the Director, or in the case of a request by a department, agency, or instrumentality of the Federal Government other than the Federal Bureau of Investigation, the head or deputy head of such department, agency, or instrumentality, within ninety days of the filing of the petition, shall either terminate the nondisclosure requirement or re-certify that disclosure may result in a danger to the national security of the United States, interference with a criminal, counterterrorism, or counterintelligence investigation, interference with diplomatic relations, or danger to the life or physical safety of any person. In the event of re-certification, the court may modify or set aside such a nondisclosure requirement if it finds that there is no reason to believe that disclosure may endanger the national security of the United States, interfere with a criminal, counterterrorism, or counterintelligence investigation, interfere with diplomatic relations, or endanger the life or physical safety of any person. If the recertification that disclosure may endanger the national security of the United States or interfere with diplomatic relations is made by the Attorney General, Deputy Attorney General, an Assistant Attorney General, or the Director of the Federal Bureau of Investigation, such certification shall be treated as conclusive unless the court finds that the recertification was made in bad faith. If the court denies a petition for an order modifying or setting aside a nondisclosure requirement under this paragraph, the recipient shall be precluded for a period of one year from filing another petition to modify or set aside such nondisclosure requirement.

(c) In the case of a failure to comply with a request for records, a report, or other information made to any person or entity under section 2709(b) of this title, section 626(a) or (b) or 627(a) of the Fair Credit Reporting Act, section 1114(a)(5)(A) of the Right to Financial Privacy Act, or section 802(a) of the National Security Act of 1947, the Attorney General may invoke the aid of any district court of the United States within the jurisdiction in which the investigation is carried on or the person or entity resides, carries on business, or may be found, to compel compliance with the request. The court may issue an order requiring the person or entity to comply with the request. Any failure to obey the order of the court may be punished by the court as contempt thereof. Any process under this section may be served in any judicial district in which the person or entity may be found.

(d) In all proceedings under this section, subject to any right to an open hearing in a contempt proceeding, the court must close any hearing to the extent necessary to prevent an unauthorized disclosure of a request for records, a report, or other information made to any person or entity under section 2709(b) of this title, section 626(a) or (b) or 627(a) of the Fair Credit Reporting Act, section 1114(a)(5)(A) of the Right to Financial Privacy Act, or section 802(a) of the National Security Act of 1947. Petitions, filings, records, orders, and subpoenas must also be kept under

seal to the extent and as long as necessary to prevent the unauthorized disclosure of a request for records, a report, or other information made to any person or entity under section 2709(b) of this title, section 626(a) or (b) or 627(a) of the Fair Credit Reporting Act, section 1114(a)(5)(A) of the Right to Financial Privacy Act, or section 802(a) of the National Security Act of 1947.

(e) In all proceedings under this section, the court shall, upon request of the government, review ex parte and in camera any government submission or portions thereof, which may include classified information.

Author Contact Information

Charles Doyle
Senior Specialist in American Public Law
cdoyle@crs.loc.gov, 7-6968